In the Next Room

or

the vibrator play

·～·

BOOKS BY SARAH RUHL AVAILABLE FROM TCG

The Clean House and Other Plays

INCLUDES:

The Clean House

Eurydice

Late: a cowboy song

Melancholy Play

Dead Man's Cell Phone

In the Next Room or the vibrator play

Passion Play

In the Next Room

or

the vibrator play

· ∾ ·

Sarah Ruhl

THEATRE COMMUNICATIONS GROUP
NEW YORK
2010

In the Next Room or the vibrator play is published by Theatre Communications Group, Inc., 520 Eighth Avenue, 24th Floor, New York, NY 10018-4156

This publication is made possible in part with public funds from the New York State Council on the Arts, a State Agency.

TCG books are exclusively distributed to the book trade by Consortium Book Sales and Distribution.

CIP data information is on file at the Library of Congress, Washington, D.C.

Book design and composition and cover design by Lisa Govan
Front cover by James McMullan

First Edition, October 2010
Third Printing, March 2014

To my husband. For the garden on Hope Street.

·❧·

In the Next Room

or

the vibrator play

·〜·

In the Next Room or the vibrator play was commissioned by and received its world premiere at Berkeley Repertory Theatre (Tony Taccone, Artistic Director; Susan Medak, Managing Director) in Berkeley, CA, in February 2009. It was directed by Les Waters; scenic design was by Annie Smart, costume design was by David Zinn, lighting design was by Russell H. Champa, sound design was by Bray Poor; the composer was Jonathan Bell, the dramaturg was Madeleine Oldham and the production stage manager was Michael Suenkel. The cast was as follows:

DR. GIVINGS	Paul Niebanck
CATHERINE GIVINGS	Hannah Cabell
SABRINA DALDRY	Maria Dizzia
MR. DALDRY	John Leonard Thompson
ANNIE	Stacy Ross
ELIZABETH	Melle Powers
LEO IRVING	Joaquín Torres

In the Next Room or the vibrator play opened on Broadway at the Lyceum Theatre in a production by Lincoln Center Theater (André Bishop, Artistic Director; Bernard Gersten, Executive Producer) on November 19, 2009. It was directed by Les Waters; scenic design was by Annie Smart, costume design was by David

Zinn, lighting design was by Russell H. Champa, sound design was by Bray Poor; the composer was Jonathan Bell and the production stage manager was Roy Harris. The cast was as follows:

DR. GIVINGS	Michael Cerveris
CATHERINE GIVINGS	Laura Benanti
SABRINA DALDRY	Maria Dizzia
MR. DALDRY	Thomas Jay Ryan
ANNIE	Wendy Rich Stetson
ELIZABETH	Quincy Tyler Bernstine
LEO IRVING	Chandler Williams

ON THE STAGE

A piano.
Closed curtains.
Knickknacks.
One chaise.
A birdcage.
A pram/bassinet.
A rocking chair.
Sumptuous rugs, sumptuous wallpaper.
Many electrical lamps, and one particularly beautiful one,
with green glass.

Next to the living room, a private doctor's room, otherwise known
as an operating theater.
The relationship between the living room and the operating theater
is all important in the design, as things happen simultaneously in
the living room and operating theater.
In the operating theater, a medical table covered with a sheet.
A basin for washing hands.
Several vibrators.
And an outlet, to plug in electrical apparatus.
One exit, in the operating theater, to an unseen room (the doctor's
private study) and one exit to the living room, which has an exit
to an unseen nursery and to the outdoors.

One might consider, rather than recorded sound, using only the live piano if one of the actors is good at playing piano.
One might consider, rather than the usual lighting instruments, something ancient.
That is to say—in a play hovering at the dawn of electricity—how should the theater itself feel?
Terribly technological or terribly primitive or neither—
At any rate, let the use of technology feel like a choice.

Personages

DR. GIVINGS, a man in his forties, a specialist in gynecological and hysterical disorders.
CATHERINE GIVINGS, his wife, a woman in her late twenties.
SABRINA DALDRY, his patient, a woman in her early thirties.
MR. DALDRY, Sabrina Daldry's husband, a man in his forties or fifties.
ANNIE, a woman in her late thirties, Dr. Givings's midwife assistant.
ELIZABETH, an African-American woman in her early thirties, a wet nurse by default.
LEO IRVING, Dr. Giving's other patient, an Englishman in his twenties or thirties.

Place

A prosperous spa town outside of New York City, perhaps Saratoga Springs.

Time

The dawn of the age of electricity; and after the Civil War; circa 1880s.

Playwright's Notes

Be sure to rehearse with a close approximation of the costumes you will be using (with the proper buttons and corsets) as the timing of dressing and undressing is all important when synchronizing with the dialogue. During simultaneous action, actors should never appear to be still or "waiting" for the other room to finish.

I am indebted to the book *The Technology of Orgasm* by Rachel P. Maines (The Johns Hopkins University Press, 1999) for inspiration. Thanks to Luke Walden for putting me on to it. Another debt is due to *AC/DC: The Savage Tale of the First Standards War* by Tom McNichol (Jossey-Bass, 2006), for thoughts on electricity. Thanks to my husband for finding it for me. Asterisks in the manuscript indicate quotations from these historical sources. A final debt is due to *A Social History of Wet Nursing in America: From Breast to Bottle* by Janet Golden (Ohio State University Press, 2001) and *Parallel Lives: Five Victorian Marriages* by Phyllis Rose (Vintage Books, 1984).

Things that seem impossibly strange in the following play are all true—such as the Chattanooga vibrator—and the vagaries of wet-nursing. Things that seem commonplace are all my own invention.

Act I

·∾·

First Scene

Mrs. Givings turns on her electric lamp.
She shows it to her baby.

MRS. GIVINGS

Look baby, it's light! No candle, no rusty tool to snuff it out, but light, pure light, straight from man's imagination into our living room. On, off, on, off, on—

She turns it off and on.

Dr. Givings enters the living room.
He walks through the space toward the operating theater without saying hello to his wife.
She watches him. After he exits:

MRS. GIVINGS

Hello.

Dr. Givings reenters the living room from the operating theater.

DR. GIVINGS

Sorry. Hello, darling.

He exits again to his office.
In the operating theater, Annie changes the sheets on the examining table.

MRS. GIVINGS

(To Dr. Givings) Hello!
(To the baby) We'll find a nice nurse for you, won't we? A nice wet nurse with lots of healthy milk. Your father put an advertisement in the paper and we'll get lots of replies today. My milk is not filling you up, is it? Are you less fat today, darling? Are your cheeks less fat?

She is near tears. She recovers.

MRS. GIVINGS

I'll find you a nurse who hasn't a child of her own. Not that I hope to find a nurse with a dead baby for that is tragic nothing is more tragic oh it hurts me here to think it—you in your pram not moving—but I suppose if I am to find a childless nurse with milk to spare, her baby must be dead, and recently dead, oh dear. I don't like to think of that.

Dr. Givings enters again.

DR. GIVINGS

I have a new patient who might ring the doorbell any second. If she arrives, would you please let Annie answer the door.

The doorbell rings.

DR. GIVINGS

Her nerves are terribly raw and it might throw off the entire clinical balance for her to meet you and the baby.

The doorbell rings.

DR. GIVINGS

Please hide.
(Shouting to his midwife)
Annie!

Mrs. Givings hides behind a piano.
Dr. Givings runs out with the pram.
Annie answers the door.

ANNIE

Hello, you must be Mr. and Mrs. Daldry, please come in.

Mr. and Mrs. Daldry enter.
Mrs. Daldry is fragile and ethereal.
Her face is covered by a veil attached to a hat.
She leans heavily on her husband's arm.

ANNIE

This way, let me show you to the operating theater—

Mrs. Daldry startles.

ANNIE

Well let's just call it the next room for now, shall we, don't be nervous, Mrs. Daldry.
Shall I just put your hat here?

9

Mrs. Daldry shakes her head.

MR. DALDRY

She's very sensitive to light.

ANNIE

Of course. Right this way.

Dr. Givings enters from the living room and overhears this last remark.
Annie turns off the electric lamp.
She leads them to the office.

DR. GIVINGS

So nice to meet you, Mrs. Daldry, Mr. Daldry. Shall I take your coat?

Mrs. Daldry shakes her head.

MR. DALDRY

She's very sensitive to cold.

DR. GIVINGS

I see. Well, have a seat. Sensitive to light, sensitive to cold—

A baby's cry is heard.

MRS. DALDRY

Oh, is there a baby here? I didn't know there was a new baby. How wonderful for you.

DR. GIVINGS

Yes. Could you shut the door please Annie?

She does so.
Then Annie sits invisibly in the corner, listening to the conversation.

Dr. Givings sits and takes out his note pad, writing down notes.
Mrs. Givings, meanwhile, in the next room, has heard the baby cry.
She sneaks out and exits to the nursery.

DR. GIVINGS

What other symptoms is your wife suffering from?

MR. DALDRY

I find her weeping at odd moments during the day, muttering
about green curtains or some such nonsense.

DR. GIVINGS

Is it nonsense, Mrs. Daldry?

MRS. DALDRY

I suppose it is. The green curtains give me terrible headache. The
color. Old ghosts in the dark.

Mr. Daldry gives Dr. Givings a pointed look.

DR. GIVINGS

Tell me more about the curtains, would you?

MRS. DALDRY

The house where I grew up my mother would wash the curtains
every week, she beat them with a stick, and there were no ghosts
in them. There was a beautiful view of a grape arbor and when the
curtains were cleaned you could see right through to the grapes,
you could almost watch them growing, they got so plump in the
autumn. My mother would make loads of jam—my mother was
not a nervous or excitable woman. It was jam, it was laughing,
and long walks out of doors. We haven't a grape arbor here—I
am full of digressions these days Dr. Givings—but the point is
I haven't the strength to wash the curtains every week and beat

the ghosts out of them. You think I am talking like a madwoman but if you could see the curtains you would see that I really am very logical. They're horrible. They're horrible.

Mr. Daldry raises his eyebrows at Dr. Givings.

DR. GIVINGS

And you have tried the usual remedies, rest and relaxation?

MRS. DALDRY

I do nothing but rest!
Nothing but rest!

MR. DALDRY

Yes.

MR. DALDRY

When I met Mrs. Daldry she was seventeen. She was an extraordinary creature. She played the piano. We ate grape jam in the arbor and there I told her I wanted to take care of her and protect her forever, didn't I.

MRS. DALDRY

Yes.

MR. DALDRY

Now I am afraid there is very little sympathy between us.

MRS. DALDRY

I am breaking his heart—. He likes me to be a certain way. Perhaps if I could play the piano again but my fingers will not work.

MR. DALDRY

No, her fingers do not work. In the living room. Or in any other room, if you take my meaning, Dr. Givings.

MRS. DALDRY

Mr. Daldry please do not embarrass me with such vulgarities.
I am shocked and disgusted and I will leave the room now.

She leaves the room.
She stands in the living room, flustered.
She sees the electrical lamp and turns it on and off.

DR. GIVINGS

Mr. Daldry, your wife is suffering from hysteria. It is a very clear
case. I recommend theraputic electrical massage—weekly—
possibly daily, we shall see—sessions. We need to relieve the pressure
of her nerves.
You will soon have your blooming wife back, she will regain her
color, light and cold will no longer have the same effect on her.
You will soon be eating grape jam and wondering how it is that
Mrs. Daldry looks so much like a seventeen year old.

MR. DALDRY

Thank you Dr. Givings. You have no idea what a source of anguish
my wife's illness has been to me. And to her, of course.

DR. GIVINGS

Of course. I will have her back for you in an hour's time.

MR. DALDRY

Thank you, Doctor.

Meanwhile, Mrs. Givings has reentered the living room with the baby.

MRS. DALDRY

(To Mrs. Givings) This lamp is extraordinary.
It hurts my eyes to watch it go on and off
but I enjoy the pain.

It is a kind of religious ecstasy to feel half blind,
do you not think?

MRS. GIVINGS

Yes, isn't it?
I was not suppposed to meet you
but I'm glad I have.
I hope you find my husband to be a comfort,
I know that I do.

MRS. DALDRY

May I hold your baby?

MRS. GIVINGS

Yes, of course.

DR. GIVINGS

I would ask you to leave Mrs. Daldry here while you take a walk around the grounds. Perhaps it's better if you don't disturb her now, Mr. Daldry.

MR. DALDRY

Of course. Whatever you think best, Doctor.

MRS. DALDRY

(While holding the baby) What is the baby's name?

MRS. GIVINGS

Letitia. Lotty for short.
Three syllables seemed like too many for a baby.

MRS. DALDRY

Lotty.

During the preceding,
Dr. Givings shakes Mr. Daldry's hand.
Mr. Daldry puts his hat on.
Mr. Daldry gives a brief quizzical glance at the vibrator.
And exits.

ANNIE
(In the living room, to Mrs. Daldry) The doctor is ready for you now.

MRS. DALDRY
Oh, no must I go back in there? I would rather hold the baby.

Mr. Daldry enters the living room.

MR. DALDRY
Be a good girl.

Mrs. Daldry hands the baby back to Mrs. Givings.

MRS. DALDRY
Oh, she's beautiful.

MRS. GIVINGS
Isn't she? Too skinny though.

Mrs. Daldry hesitates, looking at the baby.

MR. DALDRY
The doctor is waiting, Sabrina.

MRS. GIVINGS
You'll be just fine. My husband is a good doctor.
Or so I've been told.
If you'll excuse me, it's time for her nap.

Mrs. Givings exits to the nursery.
Annie leads Mrs. Daldry into the operating theater.
Mr. Daldry surveys the living room and prepares to walk the grounds.

In the operating theater:

DR. GIVINGS

Now then, Mrs. Daldry, I would ask you to remove your clothing but you may keep your underthings on. Please remove your corset, if you would. Annie will place a sheet over your lower regions. We will respect your modesty in every particular.

Mrs. Daldry nods.

DR. GIVINGS

I shall give you privacy.

He turns his back on them, a gentleman,
as Mrs. Daldry undresses with Annie's help.
Mrs. Givings has reentered the living room without the baby.
She sees Mr. Daldry.

MRS. GIVINGS

Hello again.

MR. DALDRY

Hello. They are trying to get rid of me. I am supposed to walk about the grounds.

MRS. GIVINGS

But is it not raining, Mr—?

MR. DALDRY

Daldry.
I don't know.

MRS. GIVINGS

Your name?

MR. DALDRY

No. If it is raining.

MRS. GIVINGS

Then you will have to gamble on whether or not to take an umbrella.

MR. DALDRY

Indeed.

Meanwhile, in the operating theater:

Mrs. Daldry disrobes with Annie's help.
It takes a while to disrobe as she wears a variety of layers.

In the living room, with Mr. Daldry and Mrs. Givings:

MRS. GIVINGS

There are three kinds of people. Those who use umbrellas when it is not raining; those who do not use umbrellas even when it is raining; and those who use umbrellas only and precisely while it rains. Which kind are you, Mr. Daldry?

MR. DALDRY

I use an umbrella while it is raining.

MRS. GIVINGS

That's too bad. I find people who do not use umbrellas while it is raining horribly romantic. Strolling, no *striding,* through the rain, with wet hair, looking at a drop of water on a branch.

MR. DALDRY

My wife is one of those.

MRS. GIVINGS

Oh yes! I could see that.

MR. DALDRY

It's damned annoying. I always worry she'll catch cold.

MRS. GIVINGS

But horribly romantic. My husband opens his umbrella at the merest hint of rain. And even if it does not rain, he will leave it open, stubborn as an ox, and keep walking. My husband is a scientist.

MR. DALDRY

And what sort of person are you, Mrs. Givings?

MRS. GIVINGS

Why, I don't know. My husband has always held the umbrella. Isn't that funny. I don't know at all what kind of person I am.

In the other room, Mrs. Daldry's clothes are now off to her underclothes. Annie drapes a sheet over her.

MRS. GIVINGS

I'll show you the grounds and we can use this very large umbrella and perhaps *I* will hold it and we shall see what kind of person I am. I only hope you do not get wet.

MR. DALDRY

It sounds like a madcap adventure.

Mrs. Givings and Mr. Daldry exit.

In the operating theater:

DR. GIVINGS

Are you ready for me?

ANNIE

Yes, Dr. Givings.

DR. GIVINGS

Are you warm enough? *(Mrs. Daldry nods)*
Mrs. Daldry, we are going to produce in you what is called a paroxysm. The congestion in your womb is causing your hysterical symptoms and if we can release some of that congestion and invite the juices downward your health will be restored.
Thanks to the dawn of electricity—yes, thank you Mr. Edison, I always tip my hat to Mr. Edison—a great American—I have a new instrument which I will use. It used to be that it would take me or it would take Annie—oh—hours—to produce a paroxysm in our patients and it demanded quite a lot of skill and patience. It was much like a child's game—trying to pat the head and rub the stomach at the same time—but thanks to this new electricial instrument we shall be done in a matter of minutes.

MRS. DALDRY

I—I'm afraid I don't—

DR. GIVINGS

Three minutes, sometimes five at the outer limits. Are you ready Mrs. Daldry?

She nods.
He takes out a huge vibrator.
He plugs it in.
He turns it on.

MRS. DALDRY

I am frightened.

DR. GIVINGS

Don't be frightened.

MRS. DALDRY

There is no danger of being electrocuted?

DR. GIVINGS

None at all.

He puts his arm under the sheets and
holds the vibrator to her private parts.

DR. GIVINGS

I will tell you an amusing story. Dr. Benjamin Franklin once decided to electrocute a bird for his turkey dinner on Christmas Eve. But, by mistake, he held onto the chain, completing the circuit, and couldn't let go. He described violently convulsing until he was able by sheer force of will to let go of the chain. He was perfectly fine! Do you feel calmer?

MRS. DALDRY

A little.

DR. GIVINGS

This will just take a matter of minutes.

Mrs. Daldry moans quietly.

DR. GIVINGS

It's all right, Mrs. Daldry. That's just fine.

Mrs. Daldry moans quietly.

DR. GIVINGS

Annie will hold your hand.

Annie holds her hand.

MRS. DALDRY

Oh, God in His Heaven!

She has a quiet paroxysm.
Now remember that these are the days
before digital pornography.
There is no cliché of how women are supposed to orgasm,
no idea in their heads of how they are supposed to sound when they
climax.
Mrs. Daldry's first orgasms could be very quiet,
organic, awkward, primal. Or very clinical. Or embarrassingly natural.
But whatever it is, it should not be a cliché, a camp version
of how we expect all women sound when they orgasm.
It is simply clear that she has had some kind of release.

DR. GIVINGS

That was very good, Mrs. Daldry. Is not this new instrument wonderful? Thank goodness for Benjamin Franklin and his electrical key! *(He waves the vibrator heavenward.)* Did you know they electrocuted an elephant in Coney Island last week? Marvelous. Annie will help you get dressed and you may meet Mr. Daldry on the grounds.

MRS. DALDRY

All right. And perhaps I may hold your baby again before I leave.

DR. GIVINGS

Ah, I did not realize you had met the baby. I hope that was not distracting in the middle of our session.

MRS. DALDRY

No—I liked holding her. We have not been able—

She weeps.

ANNIE

Oh, there, there.

MRS. DALDRY

—to have children. I do not know what is wrong with me.

DR. GIVINGS

Oh, dear Mrs. Daldry. Take heart. You see, Annie, it is the pent-up emotion inside the womb that causes her hysterical symptoms, you can see it quite clearly. I will administer another round of therapy to the patient. Lie back down, Mrs. Daldry.

He plugs the vibrator in again.

MRS. DALDRY

No, please no, do not touch me there again, it is very painful—no, please no— *(He places the vibrator to her private parts)* Oh—

DR. GIVINGS

What are you feeling, Mrs. Daldry?

MRS. DALDRY

My feet are very hot—dancing on hot coals—and down—down there—cold and hot to the touch—my heart is racing—

She has a quiet paroxysm.

DR. GIVINGS

That's all right, Mrs. Daldry, there there. You just lie there and stay quiet for a while. I am going to go wash my hands.

He moves to the wash basin.
She sits up.

MRS. DALDRY

(To Annie) Can you please hand me my hat.

ANNIE

Of course. You don't need to be ashamed. This instrument has quite the same effect on all of our patients. Sometimes they laugh and weep all at the same time. They often call for God.

Mrs. Daldry stands wearing her hat, with her sheet wrapped around her. Her sheet falls off as she puts on her hat and she is left only wearing her bloomers and her veil.

MRS. DALDRY

Oh dear.

ANNIE

It is quite all right Mrs. Daldry.

Annie puts the sheet back on her.

MRS. DALDRY

I am suddenly drowsy.

ANNIE

Yes, most of our patients become drowsy after the treatment.

MRS. DALDRY

Might I lie down again?

ANNIE

Please do.

MRS. DALDRY

You are a midwife?

ANNIE

Yes.

MRS. DALDRY

And you assist Dr. Givings with births and all manner of things?

ANNIE

Yes.

MRS. DALDRY

How did you come to be a midwife?

ANNIE

I was thirty-three and unmarried, and hadn't the patience for teaching young children.

MRS. DALDRY

You have assisted women in their confinements?

ANNIE

Yes.

MRS. DALDRY

So you have seen every form of torture.

ANNIE

I have seen women in a great deal of pain, yes.

MRS. DALDRY

Hold my hand and I will fall asleep.

ANNIE

Of course.

Annie holds Mrs. Daldry's hand and strokes her hair.
Mrs. Daldry falls asleep.
Throughout the next bit, she drowses, and then wakes
and gets dressed with the help of Annie.

In the other room,
Mr. Daldry and Mrs. Givings return from their walk on the grounds.
They are laughing and drenched.
Mrs. Givings shakes out her umbrella.

MRS. GIVINGS

I must be a very inconsistent person! I like to be wet and then I like to be dry and then I like to be wet again!

MR. DALDRY

You are very healthy and robust. I could barely keep up with you.

MRS. GIVINGS

I love to walk—I never had enough exercise as a child so now I walk walk walk no one can keep up with me not even Dr. Givings—that is how he fell in love with me, he said he was determined to keep up with me—he only saw the back of my head before we married because I was always one step ahead. He said he had to marry me to see my face.

Dr. Givings enters.

MRS. GIVINGS

Didn't you darling?

DR. GIVINGS

What's that?

MRS. GIVINGS

Have to marry me in order to see my face?

DR. GIVINGS

I see you have met my wife.

MR. DALDRY

Indeed.

DR. GIVINGS

We had a very successful session. You should find Mrs. Daldry much relaxed.

MR. DALDRY

Excellent.

MRS. GIVINGS

I gave Mr. Daldry a tour of the grounds. We got wet.

DR. GIVINGS

I don't want you catching cold. The baby mustn't catch cold at this age.

MRS. GIVINGS

You know I'm healthy as an ox. If only more of my milk would come in. Oh, excuse me, Mr. Daldry that is not polite to mention in mixed company.

MR. DALDRY

Are you advertising for a nurse?

MRS. GIVINGS

Indeed we are.

MR. DALDRY

Our housekeeper recently lost her baby and I believe she still has plentiful milk. Perhaps she could help though we don't want to lose her services, she is very upstanding and all the rest of it, very hard to find, a gem. Self-educated, you see, with the manners of a lady. I don't know if she'd ever take it into her head to be a wet nurse, you know what they say about wet nurses—nine parts devil, one part cow—but that's what you want, isn't it? A nice young woman who never intended to be a wet nurse but who has milk, milk to spare.

MRS. GIVINGS

Oh, she sounds perfect, we desperately want someone very moral whose child is recently dead.

MRS. GIVINGS	DR. GIVINGS
Oh, no—what I meant to say is—	What she means to say is—

MRS. GIVINGS

It's only that they say morality goes right through the milk. Mrs. Evans said just the other day, oh I wouldn't use a darkie, the morality goes right through the milk. But in the South, I don't know *what* they do in the South—

MR. DALDRY

Elizabeth our housekeeper is colored but she is very moral, very Christian. She goes to church every week with Mrs. Daldry who is a very devout woman.

MRS. GIVINGS

I see.

DR. GIVINGS

Has she recovered from the death of her child?

27

MR. DALDRY

As I said, she's a very religious woman resigned to the will of God.
And her milk is still plentiful.

MRS. GIVINGS

Darling, I don't know about a—

DR. GIVINGS

My father was a well-known abolitionist, Mr. Daldry.

MR. DALDRY

I believe I've heard of him. William Givings.

DR. GIVINGS

Yes.
(To Mrs. Givings) You'd rather have a Negro Protestant than an
Irish Catholic, wouldn't you?

Mrs. Givings thinks about that.

DR. GIVINGS

Is she married?

MR. DALDRY

Yes.

MRS. GIVINGS

That's good.

MR. DALDRY

To be sure—you don't want an unmarried woman boarding at
your house—turn the household upside down—the pretty ones
anyway—

28

He laughs and jostles Dr. Givings.
Mrs. Givings stares.
Dr. Givings clears his throat.

MR. DALDRY

That is to say—she's married to a fine man with a steady job.

DR. GIVINGS

We would be happy to take on your housekeeper Elizabeth as a
wet nurse. And we can pay handsomely but not so handsomely
that she leaves your service. We really are in dire straits because
my wife's milk is not adequate, I'm afraid. Bottle-fed babies don't
do well in cholera season, they don't do well at all. It's no time to
stand on prejudice, Catherine.

MRS. GIVINGS

My husband is a very unconventional man, a scientist. I've no idea
what the neighbors will say.

DR. GIVINGS

Let them observe that your baby is growing nice and fat.

Mrs. Daldry enters, looking wonderfully well rested.

MRS. GIVINGS

How well rested you look!

MRS. DALDRY

I feel wonderful. Your husband is a good doctor.

MRS. GIVINGS

Yes he is.

MR. DALDRY

There are roses in your cheeks.

29

DR. GIVINGS

Is the light bothering you, Mrs. Daldry?

MRS. DALDRY

No, I hardly noticed it. I was horrified when the electric lamp was invented. I so prefer candlelight and I thought, from now on people's faces will look like monsters in the evening, without the help of candlelight. No flicker, no glow. But none of you look like monsters at present, you all look very charming. You are wet, Mr. Daldry.

MR. DALDRY

It is raining, Mrs. Daldry. Shall we?

Mrs. Daldry nods.

MR. DALDRY

Might we borrow an umbrella? I did not anticipate rain.

DR. GIVINGS

To be sure. I always keep an extra umbrella in case of emergencies.

MRS. DALDRY

Thank you, Dr. Givings. I will see you again soon I hope?

DR. GIVINGS

Tomorrow, I believe is best. We will need daily sessions.

MR. DALDRY

Excellent.
(In lowered tones, away from the ladies) Oh—how much do I owe you, Doctor?

DR. GIVINGS

Not to worry. We'll settle up weekly.

MR. DALDRY

Oh fine, fine.

Then we shall see you tomorrow. And we'll bring Elizabeth with us!

DR. GIVINGS

(As they exit) Good day!

MR. AND MRS. DALDRY

Good day!

MRS. GIVINGS

Good day!

The door shuts.

MRS. GIVINGS

I'm nervous about bringing a stranger into the house, very nervous indeed.

DR. GIVINGS

Lotty is losing weight, my dear.

MRS. GIVINGS

Yes, of course, it's all my fault.

DR. GIVINGS

I'm not assigning blame, my darling.

MRS. GIVINGS

Whose fault is it then?

DR. GIVINGS

No one's. The body is blameless. Milk is without intention.

MRS. GIVINGS

A good mother has a fat child. And everyone knows it.

DR. GIVINGS

Then it will be a relief to find her a good nurse.

MRS. GIVINGS

Indeed. I cannot wait to meet her.

DR. GIVINGS

Cheer up, my darling. We are healthy and happy, are we not?

MRS. GIVINGS

(Automatically) Yes.
(Then, smiling, with sincerity) Yes.

He kisses her on the cheek and exits.
Mrs. Givings, alone.

Second Scene

Dr. Givings examines Elizabeth in the operating theater.

DR. GIVINGS

It is important to examine you to be sure your milk is healthy.

ELIZABETH

Yes, sir.

DR. GIVINGS

I also need to be sure you haven't any venereal disease that could be passed through the milk to the child. If you could just lie back please . . .

ELIZABETH

Sir, I'd rather not.

DR. GIVINGS

I'm a man of science, Elizabeth. Believe me, I won't be shocked.

ELIZABETH

Yes, sir.
Sir—you won't touch there, will you?

Mrs. Givings enters the living room.

DR. GIVINGS

I'm going to give you a medical exam, that's all.

She lies back. He covers her with a sheet.
The doorbell rings.
Mrs. Givings answers it.
Mrs. Daldry appears.

MRS. DALDRY

Hello!

MRS. GIVINGS

Hello!

MRS. DALDRY

I was walking the grounds, they're lovely.

MRS. GIVINGS

Why, you look in the bloom of health.

MRS. DALDRY

I played the piano again!

MRS. GIVINGS

What did you play?

MRS. DALDRY

I like to make songs up.

MRS. GIVINGS

Would you play one for me, please oh please?

MRS. DALDRY

I am very shy.

MRS. GIVINGS

No one is shy around me, Mrs. Daldry, I have the most wonderful effect upon shy people, they hear me talk and they think, oh why be shy?

MRS. DALDRY

I don't feel shy around you, Mrs. Givings.

MRS. GIVINGS

I knew it! You see I'm terrible at the piano, I just pick at it with one or two fingers, it's hardly been used, you must play it. The poor thing is *languishing* without a human touch. It is like a piece of dead wood without being played.

MRS. DALDRY

How can I say no?

Mrs. Daldry goes to the piano. She plays a pretty, somber, mysterious little tune.

In the next room:

DR. GIVINGS

Thank you Elizabeth, you were very brave, and you are very healthy. You can get dressed now.

Dr. Givings exits and Elizabeth gets dressed.

MRS. GIVINGS

Oh but that's beautiful! A bit sad, isn't it? Do you think we make
sad things into songs in order to hold on to the sadness or to
banish it—I think it is to banish the sadness. So then if you write
a happy song, is it not sadder than a sad song because by making
it you have banished your own happiness into a song? What do
you think?

MRS. DALDRY

I don't know.

MRS. GIVINGS

Does it have words?

MRS. DALDRY

No.

MRS. GIVINGS

Oh, but it must have words, Mrs. Daldry, oh it must. I will supply
the words, play it again, and I will sing some words with it, how
is that?

MRS. DALDRY

All right.

Mrs. Daldry plays and Mrs. Givings sings.

MRS. GIVINGS

You raise the blinds in the morning
And I like to close them at night.
Together we sleep near the birdhouse
And forget the electrical light.

Dr. Givings reenters the operating theater and escorts the now dressed Elizabeth to the living room.

MRS. DALDRY

Well that was very nice.

MRS. GIVINGS

Did you like it? Did it go with your song? Oh I hope you liked it. I hope the song liked the words because the words loved the song!

MRS. DALDRY

The song liked the words.

Dr. Givings enters with Elizabeth.

DR. GIVINGS

Mrs. Givings.

MRS. GIVINGS

Hello darling.

DR. GIVINGS

I have examined Elizabeth and she is very fit and healthy and will be a wonderful nurse to Letitia.

MRS. GIVINGS

Oh, that's marvelous! I'm so sorry about your own child, Elizabeth, that's dreadful.

ELIZABETH

Thank you.

MRS. GIVINGS

What was your child's name or did she have a name yet, oh that would be horrible, I don't know what's worse frankly, a name or no name yet, oh I need to stop talking, when death comes up I just ramble on and on, I'll stop now.

ELIZABETH

His name was Henry Douglas.

MRS. GIVINGS

A boy.

ELIZABETH

Yes.

MRS. GIVINGS

Have you—buried him yet?

ELIZABETH

He's buried at the churchyard, All Soul's. He was baptized before he died and for that I'm grateful.

MRS. GIVINGS

Oh, yes. Baptism, at least, is a comfort—he is in Heaven now.

ELIZABETH

I don't like to talk about Henry Douglas. Ma'am.

MRS. GIVINGS

No of course you wouldn't. Forgive me.

MRS. DALDRY

Elizabeth has two other boys. Two lovely boys, very well behaved.

MRS. GIVINGS

Oh, what a relief. We hope to have extra children, just in case, that
is to say, more children. I would love to have a great big brood, all
climbing over the furniture, furniture is so dead, that is to say so
lifeless, I mean so sad, without children.

MRS. DALDRY

I don't have any children.

MRS. GIVINGS

Oh! What a pity.

Mrs. Daldry is visibly agitated.

DR. GIVINGS

Elizabeth, would you like to meet the baby?

ELIZABETH

Yes, sir.

DR. GIVINGS

Catherine, please bring the baby in to Elizabeth. Mrs. Daldry,
why don't you come with me.

MRS. DALDRY

Yes, Doctor.

Mrs. Givings exits to the nursery.
Elizabeth sits, nervous. She takes off her hat.
Mrs. Daldry and Dr. Givings go to the operating theater.

DR. GIVINGS

Did that upset you to talk about children?

MRS. DALDRY

A little.

DR. GIVINGS

Are you feeling nervous?

MRS. DALDRY

My heart is pounding and I feel quite weak.

DR. GIVINGS

Well you just lie down, just lie down, and I will administer treatment.

MRS. DALDRY

Where is Annie today?

DR. GIVINGS

She should be arriving momentarily.

MRS. DALDRY

I do not wish to undress in front of you.

DR. GIVINGS

Yes, of course. I will make some notes. Call out when you are ready for me.

Dr. Givings sits at his desk.
Mrs. Daldry starts to undress.
In the living room,
Mrs. Givings enters with the baby and gives her to Elizabeth.

MRS. GIVINGS

Well. Here she is!

ELIZABETH

Would you like me to feed her now, ma'am?

MRS. GIVINGS

I suppose. She must be hungry.

Elizabeth sits, undoes her shirt, and begins nursing.
Elizabeth cries, with no sound.
Mrs. Givings watches. Mrs. Givings is on the verge of tears.
Elizabeth notices.

ELIZABETH

Perhaps it would be better if I fed her in the nursery.

MRS. GIVINGS

Yes, I think so.

ELIZABETH

Excuse me.

MRS. GIVINGS

Of course. Just through there.

Elizabeth exits to the nursery with the baby.
Mrs. Givings puts her head in her hands.
Dr. Givings enters the living room.

DR. GIVINGS

Excuse me darling—
What is it?

MRS. GIVINGS

Well, Lotty took to Elizabeth right away. She latched right on to
her breast and it made me feel very strange, to see her latched on

to another woman's breast. For once it wasn't the baby who was crying. But I feel very queer, I do.

DR. GIVINGS

Now you have to think of the baby and what's best for the baby. She would starve without milk, so think about that and be practical.

MRS. GIVINGS

I don't feel well.

MRS. DALDRY

(From the operating theater) I'm ready, Dr. Givings!

DR. GIVINGS

I have to attend to Mrs. Daldry. Why don't you have a nice lie-down. Here, I'll shut off the lamp.

He does.

MRS. GIVINGS

I don't want to lie down. I want to feed my own child.

DR. GIVINGS

But you can't, love. Your milk isn't adequate.
I love you.

He exits.
She paces around the living room.
She tries to play the song Mrs. Daldry played on the piano.
She picks at the piano with two fingers.

In the operating theater, Dr. Givings readies the vibrator.

DR. GIVINGS

Sorry for the delay.

MRS. DALDRY

Not at all.

He turns on the vibrator.
It makes a loud sound.
Mrs. Givings hears the sound, registers
its oddness, and goes on playing the piano.

DR. GIVINGS

Fine weather we're having.

MRS. DALDRY

Mm.

DR. GIVINGS

Chilly but bright.

MRS. DALDRY

Indeed.

DR. GIVINGS

There we are.

Dr. Givings puts the vibrator to Mrs. Daldry's private parts.

DR. GIVINGS

This will only take but a few minutes, Mrs. Daldry.

MRS. DALDRY

Oh . . .

DR. GIVINGS

There there. What are you feeling, Mrs. Daldry?

MRS. DALDRY

It's not working, today it's not working.

Dr. Givings adjusts the machine, making it louder.

DR. GIVINGS

There?

MRS. DALDRY

I don't know.

He repositions the machine, under the blankets.

MRS. DALDRY

Nothing. I feel nothing.

He turns it up again. The vibrating noise stops all together. And the lights go out.

DR. GIVINGS

Oh, dear.

MRS. DALDRY

Did I make it stop?

DR. GIVINGS

It's not your fault. Electrical failure.

Mrs. Givings looks up in the dark of the living room. She lights several candles.

Annie enters the operating theater.

DR. GIVINGS

Well, I'm glad you're here, Annie, we've had a power failure.

MRS. DALDRY

My head.

ANNIE

Oh, dear Mrs. Daldry, are you ill?

DR. GIVINGS

(To Annie, in low tones) I have been trying these last three minutes, it's never taken longer than three minutes with this machine.

ANNIE

Should I try the manual treatment, Dr. Givings?

DR. GIVINGS

Yes, why don't you, I will go look into this. Good day Mrs. Daldry, Annie.

MRS. DALDRY

What is the manual treatment?

ANNIE

You just lie back.

In the near dark,
Annie puts her hand under the sheet and begins to stimulate Mrs. Daldry.
We certainly do not see this, and the actress needn't simulate it exactly,
but under the sheets, Mrs. Daldry has a female ejaculation.

MRS. DALDRY

Oh! Everything is quite wet! I don't know what's happened, I'm sorry—I. How embarrassing.

ANNIE

That happens from time to time, Mrs. Daldry, I'll change the sheets.
Aristotle talked all about it.

MRS. DALDRY

Aristotle?

ANNIE

Yes.

MRS. DALDRY

Do you read Greek?

ANNIE

Yes.

MRS. DALDRY

My goodness.

ANNIE

I'm going to wash my hands.

MRS. DALDRY

Of course.

Meanwhile, in the other room, Elizabeth enters.
The living room is now lit with several candles.

ELIZABETH

Do you need me this evening, Mrs. Givings?

MRS. GIVINGS

Perhaps after supper?

ELIZABETH

All right.

Elizabeth turns to go.

MRS. GIVINGS

Wait a moment.

Elizabeth, when the milk comes in, can you feel any love for the child?

ELIZABETH

I try not to think of love. I try not to think of Henry Douglas.

MRS. GIVINGS

Of course. Do you want more children, Elizabeth? That is a tactless question, you don't need to answer, forgive me, sometimes I say whatever is in my head.

I want more children and my husband desperately wants more children but I am afraid of another birth, aren't you? When I gave birth I remember so clearly, the moment her head was coming out of my body, I thought: why would any rational creature do this twice, knowing what I know now? And then she came out and clambered right on to my breast and tried to eat me, she was so hungry, so hungry it terrified me—her hunger. And I thought: is that the first emotion? Hunger? And not hunger for *food* but wanting to eat other *people*? Specifically one's mother? And then I thought—isn't it strange, isn't it strange about Jesus? That is to say, about Jesus being a man? For it is women who are eaten— who turn their bodies into food—I gave up my blood—there was so much blood—and I gave up my body—but I couldn't feed her, could not turn my body into food, and she was *so hungry.* I suppose that makes me an inferior kind of woman and a very inferior kind of Jesus.

47

ELIZABETH

Hmm.

MRS. GIVINGS

Oh, dear, they said you were very religious, that must have
sounded—

ELIZABETH

I *was* very religious.

MRS. GIVINGS

Oh—I'm sorry, I—

ELIZABETH

I thought of Jesus while I was giving birth, like you. But I wasn't
thinking about why was He a man. I was thinking, please save me
Jesus. And He did. Now why He didn't save my Henry I don't
know, so I stopped believing in Him.

MRS. GIVINGS

Oh!

The light comes back on.
They are astonished.

MRS. GIVINGS

Ah, the electricity is back.

Mrs. Daldry enters the living room, dressed.

MRS. DALDRY

Hello.

MRS. GIVINGS

Hello!

ELIZABETH

Hello.

MRS. GIVINGS

You look refreshed.

MRS. DALDRY

Do I?

MRS. GIVINGS

Oh, yes. Would you play us something on the piano, I am sure
Elizabeth would love to hear you play.

ELIZABETH

I have to get back to my boys for supper.

MRS. GIVINGS

Oh stay for just one song.

MRS. DALDRY

All right.

Mrs. Daldry plays a little tune. It is sad.
They all listen to the song.
Elizabeth cries but no one sees her crying.
Annie enters.

ANNIE

What a pretty song, Mrs. Daldry.

MRS. DALDRY

Thank you, Annie.

ELIZABETH

I must go.

MRS. DALDRY

And I.

ANNIE

I am walking in your direction.

MRS. GIVINGS

Good-bye then, everyone gets a good walk except for me. Come again tomorrow or I will be very dull.

Elizabeth lingers.

MRS. GIVINGS

What is it, Elizabeth?

ELIZABETH

Do you pay me now, or later?

MRS. GIVINGS

Oh goodness! I haven't any money, I'll have to ask my husband. Perhaps we can settle up weekly?

ELIZABETH

That's fine. Good-bye.

MRS. GIVINGS

Good-bye.

They all exit.
Mrs. Givings blows the candles out.
Dr. Givings enters, pleased that the power is back on.

DR. GIVINGS

The power is back on! One day whole cities will be electrified. Mr. Edison is the man to do it.

MRS. GIVINGS

Don't talk to me about electricity.
You know how it bores me.
Everyone is gone.
And we are alone.

DR. GIVINGS

Indeed we are.

MRS. GIVINGS

I shall turn this off.

She kisses him.

DR. GIVINGS

Shall we go upstairs?

MRS. GIVINGS

Or stay here . . .

DR. GIVINGS

In the living room?

MRS. GIVINGS

I suppose it is for living in.

They move to the sofa, awkward.
They kiss again, with polite desire.
The doorbell rings.
They look at each other as though to say:
Don't answer that.
The doorbell rings again.

DR. GIVINGS

I'll get it.

Dr. Givings turns on the light.
Mrs. Givings blinks.
Dr. Givings answers the door.

DR. GIVINGS

Mrs. Daldry?

MRS. DALDRY

I forgot my hat.

DR. GIVINGS

You look flushed. Are you all right?

MRS. DALDRY

Perhaps the walk overexcited me. I am not used to walking that much in one day. Annie and I were walking rather quickly, and discussing—well—she knows *Greek,* can you imagine—I feel faint.

Mrs. Daldry half collapses on the arm of a chair.
Dr. Givings goes to her.

MRS. GIVINGS

Oh!

DR. GIVINGS

There, there Mrs. Daldry. Why don't you come see me in the operating theater. The electricity is back on.

MRS. DALDRY

Perhaps I'm intruding on your domestic life.

DR. GIVINGS

Not at all.

MRS. GIVINGS

Not at all.

DR. GIVINGS

This way. Mrs. Givings, why don't you go to the nursery.

MRS. GIVINGS

Yes, dear.

Dr. Givings and Mrs. Daldry go into the operating theater.
Mrs. Givings listens at the door.

DR. GIVINGS

No need to undress all the way, as you're not feeling well, just lie
down gently. Are you still feeling faint?

MRS. DALDRY

A little.

She takes her gloves off.

DR. GIVINGS

Are you often subject to faintness?

MRS. DALDRY

No more than once a week, I daresay.

DR. GIVINGS

I see. We'll set you to rights, no worries.
Are you ready?

She nods.
He puts the vibrator down her bloomers.
Mrs. Givings listens at the door.

MRS. DALDRY

Oh. Oh. No.

Mrs. Givings cocks her head.

DR. GIVINGS

Tell me what you're feeling.

MRS. DALDRY

I don't—want—a machine.

DR. GIVINGS

Any fluid, Mrs. Daldry?

MRS. DALDRY

No. Nothing.

DR. GIVINGS

I will try using a finger as well as the instrument to replicate Annie's experiment. Vulvular massage has been discounted in many circles but occasionally with the proper diagnosis and method it is just the thing.

He puts his hand under the sheets.

MRS. DALDRY

Oh, oh, oh!

DR. GIVINGS

There, there, Mrs. Daldry, let it all out.

MRS. DALDRY

Oh, Annie!

DR. GIVINGS

Excuse me?

MRS. DALDRY

Please leave me. I feel much relieved.

DR. GIVINGS

I will wash up and let you get sorted. Take your time.

Mrs. Givings knocks at the door of the operating theater.

DR. GIVINGS

(To Mrs. Daldry) Excuse me.

He opens the door and finds Mrs. Givings there.

DR. GIVINGS

(To Mrs. Givings) What is it? The baby?

MRS. GIVINGS

What is that sound? What were you doing?

DR. GIVINGS

Electrical therapy, my dear. Very successful session.

MRS. GIVINGS

I wish to see it.

DR. GIVINGS

You would not understand. Leave me my dry boring science and I will give you the rest of the world. You said yourself that my electricity bored you.

MRS. GIVINGS

I insist on seeing your machine now.

DR. GIVINGS

Are you going to force me to lock my laboratory?

MRS. GIVINGS

I am your wife.

DR. GIVINGS

And happily you are my blooming young wife without a hint of neurosis and in no need of my inventions or experiments.

MRS. GIVINGS

Experiment on me!

DR. GIVINGS

I can assure you that you would not like it.

MRS. GIVINGS

Experiment on me!

DR. GIVINGS

It would be unseemly for a man of science to do experiments on his wife. I'd lose my credibility. Now would you have the good grace to be quiet while Mrs. Daldry is in the next room—

Mrs. Daldry enters the living room, looking the very picture of health.

MRS. DALDRY

Do not let me forget my hat again.

MRS. GIVINGS

(Quickly) It is right here.

MRS. DALDRY

Ah. Thank you Dr. Givings.

56

Mrs. Givings hands Mrs. Daldry her hat.

DR. GIVINGS

Not at all. Good-bye.

MRS. DALDRY

Good-bye.

MRS. GIVINGS

Good-bye.

Mrs. Daldry exits.

DR. GIVINGS

I'm going to the club. Mr. Edison's man is electrocuting dogs this evening. He is out to prove the deadliness of the alternating current over and above direct current. I think it's hogwash. In alternating current, the current flips back and forth, back and— you see how much this bores you.

He locks the door of the operating theater and puts the key in his pocket.

MRS. GIVINGS

Yes it is very boring good-bye and don't kiss me good-bye please.

DR. GIVINGS

Very well.

He leaves.
She storms.
She goes toward the operating theater.
She jiggles the door.
The living room doorbell rings.
She answers the door.

57

MRS. DALDRY

I've forgotten my gloves, I'm so sorry, what must you think of me.

MRS. GIVINGS

Oh, I'm so happy to see you! My husband has just gone to the club and I am bored out of my mind.

MRS. DALDRY

I think my gloves are in the other room.

MRS. GIVINGS

It is locked.

MRS. DALDRY

Oh, I can come back tomorrow for my gloves.

MRS. GIVINGS

No, please stay. I have developed the most insatiable curiosity about my husband's operating theater. Perhaps you can tell me how it works.

MRS. DALDRY

Oh—no—I don't know how it works—

MRS. GIVINGS

He plugs it in, he turns it on, and then?

MRS. DALDRY

He applies electrical current to my—to my body—to release the magnetic fluid. That is what he says. Because there is excess fluid in my womb, causing my hysterical symptoms.

MRS. GIVINGS

Fluid?

MRS. DALDRY

Yes.

Really, I must go now—

MRS. GIVINGS

You sounded like this: oh, oh, ah-ee!

MRS. DALDRY

You were listening?

MRS. GIVINGS

It was loud.

MRS. DALDRY

Oh, dear. I will leave you now.

MRS. GIVINGS

Stay for tea.

Where does my husband place the electrical device?

MRS. DALDRY

(Pointing vaguely to her knees) Just here.

MRS. GIVINGS

Hm.

And does it give you a pleasurable or a painful sensation?

MRS. DALDRY

Pleasure, and pain all at once—electrical current runs through my
entire body—I see light—patterns of light, under my eyelids—
and a kind of white-hot coal on my feet—and I shudder violently,
as though struck by a terrible lightning—and then a darkness
descends, and I want to sleep.

MRS. GIVINGS

I never heard of anything so strange.

MRS. DALDRY

Let's talk of other things. They electrocuted an elephant at Coney
Island.

MRS. GIVINGS

Yes, I've heard.

MRS. DALDRY

It is getting dark.

MRS. GIVINGS

I will turn the lamp on.

MRS. DALDRY

Please, don't.

They sit in the dark.

MRS. DALDRY

Can you imagine a time when all will be electric, all will be plugged
in, why it will not stop at lights, but the way we cook our eggs
and the way we get our chickens to lay their eggs too. Mr. Edison
invented a recording device which he says will change everything,
it will record the last wishes of the dying. Can you imagine? A man
may know the voice of his great-great-grandfather, may know his
last wishes. And what will become of the human body? Electrical
arms perhaps. Even the fireflies will become electric.

MRS. GIVINGS

Electrical fireflies.

MRS. DALDRY

Yes.

MRS. GIVINGS

Electrical pianos.

MRS. DALDRY

God forbid.

MRS. GIVINGS

Oh, to think of never carrying a candle! Not to walk through a hallway at night, holding a candle, afraid of tripping in the dark, starting a fire—it makes one more solemn, do you not think? Or to blow out a candle—how beautiful! With one's own breath, to extinguish the light! Do you think our children's children will be less solemn? A flick of the finger—and all is lit! A flick of the finger, and all is dark! On, off, on off! We could change our minds a dozen times a second! On, off, on off! We shall be like gods!

MRS. DALDRY

I'm afraid so.

MRS. GIVINGS

Have you a hat pin?

MRS. DALDRY

Yes.

She hands Mrs. Givings a pin from her hat.
Mrs. Givings goes to pick the lock of the operating theater.

MRS. GIVINGS

I will just retrieve your gloves.

Mrs. Givings enters the operating theater.
Mrs. Daldry is on her heels.
Mrs. Givings looks around.

MRS. GIVINGS

Is this it?

MRS. DALDRY

Yes.

MRS. GIVINGS

How extraordinary. It looks like a farming tool.
Where do you put it?

MRS. DALDRY

Here.

Mrs. Givings puts the vibrator to her private parts, over her skirt.

MRS. GIVINGS

I see.
Where's the switch?

MRS. DALDRY

I've no idea.

Mrs. Givings finds the switch.
The vibrator turns on.

MRS. GIVINGS

What a sound!

MRS. DALDRY

I will hold it in place for you.

She does, over Mrs. Givings's skirts.

MRS. GIVINGS

Is it heavy?

MRS. DALDRY

Tolerably.

MRS. GIVINGS

Well I don't see what all the fuss is about.

MRS. DALDRY

Sometimes I close my eyes.

Mrs. Givings closes her eyes.
Mrs. Daldry gently puts the vibrator under Mrs. Givings's skirt.
The buzz of the vibrator, for longer than is comfortable.

MRS. GIVINGS

Oh!
Oh!

Mrs. Givings climaxes.
And as she does so, she weeps.

MRS. GIVINGS

Well that was very awful—it was a very dreadful strange feeling,
I see why he has been keeping it from me.

MRS. DALDRY

Yes.

MRS. GIVINGS

Would you like a go?

MRS. DALDRY

Oh, no only the doctor can administer the treatment.

MRS. GIVINGS

I don't see why. It looks quite simple. In this day and age, all one has to know how to do is press a button or pull a switch. I'll hold it for you.

MRS. DALDRY

All right. Wait— *(She listens)*
Is that not your husband's carriage?

MRS. GIVINGS

I can't hear a thing.

MRS. DALDRY

I hear horse's hooves.

MRS. GIVINGS

You're imagining things. He won't be home from the club until at least seven o'clock.

MRS. DALDRY

Are you sure?

MRS. GIVINGS

Oh yes, when he starts talking about electricity he cannot stop.

MRS. DALDRY

Well then.

MRS. GIVINGS

Are you ready?

MRS. DALDRY

I think so.

MRS. GIVINGS

Here we go!

Mrs. Givings puts the vibrator to Mrs. Daldry's private parts.
They look heavenward.
The steady hum of the vibrator. Transcendent music.
A curtain falls.

Act II

·❧·

First Scene

Two weeks or so later.
Dr. Givings and Leo,
in the operating theater.

LEO

And then she left, very abruptly, for Italy.

DR. GIVINGS

I see.

LEO

It was a terrible shock.
I had been studying in Florence for the year. They are exacting masters over there—the line must be just so—the proportion just so—there is no freedom—you sharpen your pencil with a knife, as Leonardo sharpened his pencil. It was heaven. Not to have freedom. No freedom in art, but in life, life! The peaches

there tasted like peaches, the rain like rain. I met the woman in question in Florence. A very beautiful woman. (I know. No one ever said: I fell in love with a woman in Italy—a very ugly woman.) But she *was* beautiful. Perhaps not classically, but never mind . . . We met at the Uffizi. She was looking at the sculptures with no embarrassment, no embarrassment at all. I painted her face all summer. When she kissed she kissed with her whole body, not like American women who kiss only with their lips.

DR. GIVINGS

Mm.

LEO

You are perhaps shocked, Doctor, that I kissed her before marriage. I am a devotee of nature and I wished to avoid the fate of my boyhood friend. On his wedding night he was repulsed by his wife's body. He said, when she disrobed for the first time, he saw something monstrous. What, what? I asked. She had body hair, he said, down there! Like a beast! You see, he had seen the female form only in marble statues—no body hair! You are a scientist, that must amuse you.

DR. GIVINGS

What men do not observe because their intellect prevents them from seeing would fill many books.

LEO

Indeed.

DR. GIVINGS

What happened to your friend?

LEO

He is now a very famous art critic.

His marriage went unconsummated for three years and was then anulled. I did not wish such a fate for myself, and so, while lips were willing and free and soft, I kissed them. Oh yes, I kissed them.

She did not come from a good family and her English was not very good but I did not care. Her soul lept out of her eyes. When I painted her I felt I could paint souls. Her soul hovered, just here, and I could see it. *(He gestures to a place about two inches from the eyes.)* So when I painted I painted two inches away from the eyes, not the eyes themselves—it was a revelation! —I digress.

Mrs. Givings enters the other room and arranges tea things.

LEO

She journeyed with me to England to meet my parents, to announce the engagement. And then, the following morning, she fled. Back to Italy! No word, no letter! No answer to my inquiries! Nothing! And my whole body revolted against me. Headaches, eyesight, weakness, nausea . . .

DR. GIVINGS

And this weakness has persisted, for, what—?

LEO

Nine months.

DR. GIVINGS

In your extremities?

LEO

Yes. But the weakness in my eyes is perhaps the worst, because of my inability to paint.

DR. GIVINGS

So you haven't painted for nine months?

LEO

You can't paint in the dark.

DR. GIVINGS

It is very rare, a case of hysteria in a man, but of course we do see it.

LEO

Is it treatable?

DR. GIVINGS

I believe it is. I'd like you to undress to your underthings and lie down on the table. Annie, my assistant, will be in shortly.

Elizabeth enters the living room with the baby.

LEO

I did not know there would be a lady in attendance.

DR. GIVINGS

She is the soul of tact and reserve.

Leo undresses.

Meanwhile, in the living room:

MRS. GIVINGS

(To Elizabeth) Was she a good eater?

ELIZABETH

An angel.

MRS. GIVINGS

Thank you, Elizabeth.

ELIZABETH

I think that babies are angels when they drink only milk, that first year. They could fly right back to where they came from, to the milk in the clouds. When they get teeth it is the beginning of the end, they become animals and there's no going back.

MRS. GIVINGS

Yes.

ELIZABETH

But this one's still an angel, no teeth.

Elizabeth touches the baby's cheek.
The baby smiles.
Mrs. Givings is jealous.

MRS. GIVINGS

Well.
That will be all now, Elizabeth.

ELIZABETH

I'll just get my things.

Elizabeth exits to the nursery.
Leo is now undressed and Dr. Givings enters the operating theater.
Annie drapes a sheet over Leo.
Mrs. Givings alone with the baby, in the living room.

MRS. GIVINGS

No smile?
You were smiling for Elizabeth.

(Singing quietly to the baby)

You raise the blinds in the morning
And I like to close them at night
Together we sleep near the birdhouse
And forget the electrical light.

In the operating theater:

DR. GIVINGS

This, Leo, is what I call the Chattanooga vibrator. My own invention.
It slips into the anal cavity.

LEO

Indeed.

DR. GIVINGS

Just face that direction, and curl up a bit, hugging your knees into
your chest.
Annie will just operate the foot pedal which controls the speed.
It functions—much like a sewing machine.

LEO

Ah.

Dr. Givings plugs the vibrator in.

DR. GIVINGS

We are going to stimulate the prostate gland. Are you ready?

LEO

I think so.

He puts the vibrator down Leo's underthings.
Annie assists.

Leo looks troubled.
Leo looks shocked.
Leo has an anal paroxysm.

LEO

Oh.
Oh!
Oh.

Mrs. Givings goes to the door—a man's voice?

DR. GIVINGS

Excellent! I think we can stop now for the day.
How are you feeling?
Would you like a cup of tea?

LEO

I would love a cup of tea.

Dr. Givings enters the living room.

MRS. GIVINGS

Hello, darling. How is *work*?

DR. GIVINGS

A new patient. An interesting case. Very rare.

MRS. GIVINGS

A man?

DR. GIVINGS

How did you know?

MRS. GIVINGS

I heard a man's voice.

73

DR. GIVINGS

I did not know the door was quite so porous.

MRS. GIVINGS

But why would a man come to see you?

DR. GIVINGS

Hysteria is very rare in a man, but then again, he is an artist.
Perhaps you should take the baby for a walk, so that you don't
chance running into him.

MRS. GIVINGS

I believe the baby is still hungry—I'll just go and find Elizabeth.

DR. GIVINGS

Yes.

She exits with the baby. Dr. Givings pours tea.
Meanwhile Leo has gotten dressed with Annie's assistance.

LEO

Thank you.
(Looking at the vibrator) How odd.

Dr. Givings enters and hands Leo tea.

LEO

Lovely.

DR. GIVINGS

I'll see you tomorrow. I believe daily sessions will be best at this
early stage.
Feel free to use the grounds.

LEO

Excellent. Thank you, Doctor.

Leo hesitates, befuddled.

DR. GIVINGS

Of course. See you tomorrow then.

LEO

Yes, yes, of course.

Leo enters the living room
at the exact moment that Mrs. Givings enters without the baby.

MRS. GIVINGS

Hello.

LEO

Hello.

MRS. GIVINGS

Mrs. Givings.

LEO

You are the doctor's wife?

MRS. GIVINGS

I am. He seldom has men here. What a rare treat to make your
acquaintance!

*She looks at him, puzzled, remembering her own experience with the
vibrator and wondering how on earth it is used on men.*

LEO

Leonard Irving.

75

MRS. GIVINGS

Pleased to meet you, Mr. Irving.

LEO

And you.

He kisses her hand.

MRS. GIVINGS

So old fashioned.

LEO

I'm afraid everyone goes around these days saying: I am a modern
man, I am a modern woman, it's the modern age, after all. But
I detest modernity.

MRS. GIVINGS

Do you! How contrary. Are you a very contrary person?

LEO

Some might say so.

MRS. GIVINGS

The cut of your coat is very old fashioned.

LEO

It's my father's old coat. I can't be bothered with the cut of a coat.
I throw on whatever my father leaves for rags.

Leo looks at the lamp and squints.

MRS. GIVINGS

Is the lamp too much for your eyes?

LEO

The light has troubled me greatly for the past nine months, but I feel better presently.

She shuts the lamp off.

MRS. GIVINGS

Just in case.

LEO

When Edison's light came out, they were all saying, my God!—light like the sunset of an Italian autumn . . . no smoke, no odor, a light without flame, without danger!* But to me, Mrs. Givings, a light without flame isn't divine—a light without flame—is like—

MRS. GIVINGS

What?

LEO

I cannot say.

MRS. GIVINGS

Why not?

LEO

I hardly know you. I would offend your feminine sensibilities.

MRS. GIVINGS

Oh, no need to be shy around me, I just blurt anything out.

LEO

Well, then light without flame is like having relations with a prostitute. No flame of love or desire, only the outer trappings of—

77

the act. And without love—without the mental quickening—the eyes—the blood—without the heart—or intellect—bodies are meat. Meat and bone and levers and technicalities.

MRS. GIVINGS

Well perhaps you were right. Perhaps you ought not to have said.

LEO

Not that I've ever known any prostitutes—intimately—

MRS. GIVINGS

(Overlapping with intimacy) I wasn't implying—

LEO

It's only a metaphor—

MRS. GIVINGS

Of course.

It is awkward.
They sit there, in the gathering darkness.

LEO

I love this time of afternoon, when the world is becoming dark, and you can see outside your window—lights in the neighboring windows coming on. One yellow—one almost white—little squares of light, other people's lives—sheltered against the night, so hopeful. Ridiculous, isn't it, to have so much hope, to think a little square of light could blot out the darkness—and yet—another comes on—and see—

He brings her to the window and shows her.

MRS. GIVINGS

Yes—one—then two—

LEO

Look—there—another window lit—golden—the rest of the house dark—an incomplete painting. I love incomplete paintings— why do painters always *insist* upon finishing paintings? It's unaccountable—*life is not like that!*

MRS. GIVINGS

Oh!

LEO

And the ones *Michelangelo* never finished—do you know them?—ghosts of lines hovering in the background. Have you ever seen *Virgin and Child with the Angels?*

MRS. GIVINGS

I have never been to Italy.

LEO

Oh you must go, and upon arrival, you must go directly to see that painting—the incomplete lines of God—they cannot be filled in because they would be too beautiful, they would shock the senses, and so they are *almost there*—women or angels—exchanging confidences—coming into being. A woman who is two-thirds done is nearer to God! A young woman on the verge of knowing herself is the most attractive thing on this earth to a man for this very reason.

MRS. GIVINGS

Do you think so?

LEO

Oh, yes.

They sit for a moment in the dark.
The doorbell rings.

79

MRS. GIVINGS

Excuse me.

Mrs. Givings jumps
and answers the door.
It is Mrs. Daldry.

MRS. GIVINGS

Mrs. Daldry!

MRS. DALDRY

Hello. Am I early? I think that I am early.

MRS. GIVINGS

I have just made the acquaintance of Mr. Irving.

MRS. DALDRY

Pleased to meet you.
But you are in the dark.

Mrs. Givings switches on the lamp.
Leo is riveted by Mrs. Daldry's fragile beauty in the light.

LEO

I must go. A thousand paintings. That is to say—a thousand apologies, as it were, for my rudeness at leaving so suddenly, I now have a thousand paintings to make. A bolt from the blue! I must order a new canvas. Several. Immediately. Good-bye.

He runs out the door.

MRS. GIVINGS

What an interesting young man.

MRS. DALDRY

Yes.

MRS. GIVINGS

A painter.

MRS. DALDRY

Indeed!

Mrs. Givings makes sure they are alone.

MRS. GIVINGS

Mrs. Daldry, I have been wanting to speak to you ever since our adventure with the hat pin. You told me that you saw light when my husband treats you, and then you got drowsy and wanted to sleep. Well, I had such different sensations I wonder if it can be the same instrument at all. I was not the least bit drowsy afterwards. In fact, I was overcome by the desire to walk, or run, or climb a tree! How could one device cause such opposite reactions. Perhaps it is because I am well and you are ill.

MRS. DALDRY

I do not know. I have been so worried that your husband might find out and get upset with us and suspend the treatment.

MRS. GIVINGS

I do not care. I am determined to use the device again and unlock the mystery as to why it makes you drowsy and makes me very excitable. Why, I feel like a scientist!

Dr. Givings enters.

DR. GIVINGS

Ah, Mrs. Daldry, Mrs. Givings. We are ready for you in the next room.

MRS. DALDRY

Yes.

Dr. Givings shoots a look at Mrs. Givings for speaking with his patient.
He guides Mrs. Daldry to the operating theater.

DR. GIVINGS

Right this way.
Looking well, looking well. Your appetite has improved, no?

MRS. DALDRY

I daresay it has.

DR. GIVINGS

Wonderful!

They go into the operating theater.
Mrs. Givings watches them go.
The doorbell rings.
Mrs. Givings answers it.

LEO

I'm sorry, I forgot my scarf.
I left in such a state.

MRS. GIVINGS

I am very glad you have returned, Mr. Irving. I am all by myself
as Mrs. Daldry has gone in to get electrical therapy and I, the wife,
am left to my own *devices*. As it were.

LEO

I'm not sure what you mean, Mrs. Givings.

MRS. GIVINGS

Have some more tea.

82

She pours.

LEO

I don't want to impose.

MRS. GIVINGS

You'll have to wait for them to finish before you can retrieve your
scarf. Sit.
Sugar?

LEO

No thank you. Sugar is for women and small fat boys.
Lovely.

In the operating theater:

Dr. Givings plugs in the vibrator while Mrs. Daldry gets undressed.
The sound of the vibrator. Leo and Mrs. Givings talk over it.

MRS. GIVINGS

It's fine weather we're having for November.

LEO

Yes. Though dark.

MRS. GIVINGS

Yes, it is dark.

Mrs. Daldry moans from the other room.
Leo speaks more loudly.

LEO

Dark so early. Dark and the trees so tall and naked. I think
November is the tallest month because when the trees have lost
their leaves they look so much taller. Tall in a—lonely way.

Mrs. Daldry moans.

LEO

Yes—November is a tall month—October is a round month—
April is a—skinny month—

MRS. GIVINGS

Oh do stop talking of the seasons!

LEO

Excuse me?

MRS. GIVINGS

We talk, we talk, and we surround ourselves with plants, with
teapots, with little statuettes to give ourselves a feeling of home, of
permanency, as if with enough heavy objects, perhaps the world
won't shatter into a million pieces, perhaps the house will not
fly away, but I experienced something the other day, Mr. Irving,
something to shatter a statuette, to shatter an elephant. Here is my
riddle: what is a thing that can put a man to death and also bring
him back to life again. Will you answer?

LEO

That is easy.

MRS. GIVINGS

Is it?

LEO

Love.

MRS. GIVINGS

No. Electricity.

84

Meanwhile, Mrs. Daldry has a loud paroxysm in the next room.

DR. GIVINGS

Very good, Mrs. Daldry.

Leo and Mrs. Givings look at each other.
Elizabeth enters with her coat.

ELIZABETH

She ate again and now she's sleeping. I never had a girl. When she eats, she eats so quietly, so politely, not like my boys, who were ravenous.

MRS. GIVINGS

Why thank you Elizabeth.

LEO

You are the baby's nurse?

ELIZABETH

(To Leo) Oh, excuse me, I did not see you—I would not have spoken of— Yes, I am the baby's nurse.

LEO

I should like to paint you nursing the baby.

ELIZABETH

That would not be—

LEO

A Madonna for our times. A Madonna after the Civil War—

ELIZABETH

Sir.

LEO

Oh dear, have I displeased you?

MRS. GIVINGS

You'll have to excuse us, Elizabeth, the men in my household are very unorthodox, artists and scientists don't care at all about convention, do they?

LEO

Since your husband has been treating me, I feel full of the most wild creative energies. I could paint all night, and everyone seems full of beauty. You, Elizabeth, are beautiful and you ought to be in a painting.

ELIZABETH

I've never had a man in the room when I've nursed a baby. My husband of course has seen me nurse my own but that is different.

LEO

I would pay you handsomely. And during your regular work hours, just triple the salary, and pretend I am not there while you work.

ELIZABETH

Triple the salary?

LEO

Yes. I cannot imagine she pays you very much for your services.

MRS. GIVINGS

Mr. Irving, really—

LEO

I will pay you ten dollars an hour for your services.

Elizabeth and Mrs. Givings look at each other, shocked. (Ten dollars was the equivalent of one hundred and seventy-five dollars or so.)

ELIZABETH

I will sit for you. But do not tell my husband and please disguise my features. And so that nothing would seem improper, I would like Mrs. Givings to sit in the room with us.

LEO

You must have a beautiful dress to wear, or a robe. Have you a dressing gown we could borrow?

MRS. GIVINGS

I—

LEO

It must be something that will allow the breast out, so that she may give suck.

Mrs. Givings is shocked.
Mrs. Daldry and Dr. Givings enter.

DR. GIVINGS

Hello, Leo. I do not like that my patients should be scheduled so that they meet up—I'm so sorry—

LEO

I left my scarf.

DR. GIVINGS

Ah, go right ahead and get it, we are finished.

MRS. DALDRY

(To Leo) Hello.

LEO

Hello.

The doorbell rings. It is Mr. Daldry.

DR. GIVINGS

Hello, Mr. Daldry.

MR. DALDRY

Doctor.

LEO

I will just fetch my scarf.

In the other room Leo looks at the vibrating machine. He wonders how it might be used on a woman.

MR. DALDRY

You are looking well, Mrs. Daldry. You looked well this morning but you have even more color in your cheeks now.

DR. GIVINGS

Isn't the improvement amazing?

MR. DALDRY

Indeed! I think she might be ready to stop treatments.

MRS. DALDRY

I think that would be premature. I am not cured yet.

MR. DALDRY

But much improved.

DR. GIVINGS

Yes.

MR. DALDRY

You are a magician, Doctor.

Leo enters the living room.

LEO

I'd forgotten my scarf.

DR. GIVINGS

Leo Irving.

MR. DALDRY

Dick Daldry.

LEO

Pleased to meet you.

MR. DALDRY

I am glad you found your scarf. It's snowing.

MRS. GIVINGS

Oh! Is it?

MRS. DALDRY

In November?

MR. DALDRY

Indeed. I brought your mackintosh, my dear.

MRS. DALDRY

Thank you.

MR. DALDRY

Thank you, Doctor.

DR. GIVINGS

Not at all.

LEO

I will follow you out, we can all walk together.

Mrs. Daldry, Mr. Daldry, Elizabeth and Leo leave.

DR. GIVINGS

Good-bye.

MRS. DALDRY

Good-bye.

MR. DALDRY

Good-bye.

ELIZABETH

Good-bye.

LEO

Good-bye.

MRS. GIVINGS

Good-bye!

Dr. Givings shuts the door.
Mrs. Givings looks disquieted.

DR. GIVINGS

What is it?

MRS. GIVINGS

I think we ought to let Elizabeth go.

DR. GIVINGS

Whatever for?
Letitia is blooming and rosy and positively fat.

MRS. GIVINGS

I think Elizabeth is becoming attached to the baby.

DR. GIVINGS

You want her to give love to the baby but not too much love.

MRS. GIVINGS

Precisely.

DR. GIVINGS

I shall never understand women.

MRS. GIVINGS

I am still leaking bits of gray milk. It is as though my body is crying.

DR. GIVINGS

Oh, darling. You'll be back to normal in no time. And it's good for
you to give up nursing, we can have another child more quickly.

MRS. GIVINGS

Another child! I can harldly—!
She won't even look at me!

DR. GIVINGS

Who?

MRS. GIVINGS

The baby!
She won't smile at me!
I am not a good mother. I do nothing! I pour the tea!
I wish you to use your machine on me.

DR. GIVINGS

Darling, it's for women who are ill. It would probably have no effect on you at all, as you're perfectly healthy.

MRS. GIVINGS

I am not healthy. I feel restless, and excitable, and I cry at the smallest thing. You help countless other women but me, your wife, you pat on the head.

DR. GIVINGS

What is the matter?

MRS. GIVINGS

She knows where to get comfort and love, and it is not from me.

DR. GIVINGS

You are her mother!

MRS. GIVINGS

In name only.
Milk is comfort, milk is love.
How will she learn to love me?

DR. GIVINGS

You do seem to be suffering, perhaps from the excess fluid of milk. I can perhaps try the treatment on you although it makes me nervous. But don't go round telling your friends. It must not get out in the scientific community that I am treating my own wife.

MRS. GIVINGS

Now?

DR. GIVINGS

I haven't any other patients for an hour.

MRS. GIVINGS

Now that you've given way I feel quite frightened.

DR. GIVINGS

There's nothing to be frightened of, darling, come along, I'll show you.

He leads her to the operating theater.

DR. GIVINGS

First you undress to your underthings. I shall turn around.

MRS. GIVINGS

Do all the women undress to their underthings?

DR. GIVINGS

It's medicine, my love.

She starts to undress and realizes
there are too many buttons in the back.

MRS. GIVINGS

I can't do this bit without your help.

DR. GIVINGS

Oh—sorry.

He helps her with the buttons and then turns around again, a gentleman.

DR. GIVINGS

Is that all right?

MRS. GIVINGS

Yes.

She finishes undressing herself.
He plugs in the vibrator.

DR. GIVINGS

Don't be alarmed.
Just lie down and relax.

She does.

DR. GIVINGS

Are you quite comfortable?

MRS. GIVINGS

Yes.

He holds the vibrator to her private parts, his face impassive.

DR. GIVINGS

Electricity is not to be feared—it is harnessed from nature.
I remember, when I was a child, I was stroking the cat's back one
day and was startled to see sparks rising up out of her fur. My
father said, this is nothing but electricity, the same thing you see
on the trees in a storm. My mother seemed alarmed. Stop stroking
the cat. You might start a fire. I kept on stroking the cat. I thought:
is nature a cat? If so, who strokes its back? God?*

MRS. GIVINGS

(With some difficulty speaking) And what did you determine?

DR. GIVINGS

Natural law.
Is that too much pressure?

MRS. GIVINGS

No.
Oh,
Oh,
Oh—
Kiss me, darling, kiss me.

DR. GIVINGS

Afterwards.

MRS. GIVINGS

No, kiss me now.
Kiss me and hold the instrument there, just there, at the same time.

DR. GIVINGS

Darling, no—that would be—

MRS. GIVINGS

I don't care, do it, do it, I have been longing to kiss someone. Like this.

She kisses him passionately
and puts the vibrator back on her private parts.

DR. GIVINGS

This is what I feared. In a sick woman the device restores balance, but in a healthy woman it makes you excitable and perhaps even causes some perverse kind of onanism.

MRS. GIVINGS

What is onanism?

DR. GIVINGS

I am relieved that you do not know. I'm afraid the experiment was not a success dear.

MRS. GIVINGS

And I say it *was* a success! Kiss me, kiss me now!

He kisses her politely.

MRS. GIVINGS

This is inadequate! You are inadequate! Oh, God!

She has not yet had a paroxysm.
He takes the vibrator away from her.

DR. GIVINGS

I made a terrible mistake bringing you into the operating theater. Men of science should never mix their family lives and their medical lives. It was my mistake, my darling, and we will both forget about it.

He unplugs the vibrator.

DR. GIVINGS

Now I want you to go upstairs and take a nap.

MRS. GIVINGS

No!

DR. GIVINGS

Catherine.

She dresses and Dr. Givings helps her with the innumerable buttons.

MRS. GIVINGS

I shall take a walk. Will you help me on with this—*for God's sake why does it have so many buttons?*

DR. GIVINGS

There *are* quite a lot of buttons.

MRS. GIVINGS

I could walk walk walk all night in the snow.

DR. GIVINGS

Is it snowing out?

MRS. GIVINGS

You didn't notice the first snow? My God. When I first met you and was nothing more than a girl I wrote my name in the snow outside your window—I would have done anything for you to notice me—you were older, and seemed so wise, so calm—and so marvelously indifferent to me. I don't know if you ever saw—it melted—no matter, if you saw my name in the snow all you'd see was a natural substance—

DR. GIVINGS

Catherine.

MRS. GIVINGS

I'm afraid you've done up the buttons wrong.

DR. GIVINGS

Sorry.

He starts doing the buttons over again.

MRS. GIVINGS

It was an unnecessary gesture, childish, a name in the snow, but a gift must be unnecessary—for it to be good—but you want it to be *useful,* you wouldn't say—well, it's useless—but you made it for me alone. And so it will never melt. It will exist for all time. Uuugh—how ridiculous I sound. My hat please.

She is dressed.

DR. GIVINGS

I made a very bad mistake today and I am sorry.

He tries to touch her.

MRS. GIVINGS

Good-bye!

She leaves the operating theater.
She leaves the house without her coat, hat or mittens.

DR. GIVINGS

Take your wrap! It's cold!
Did you really write your name in the snow?

Dr. Givings, alone.
He washes up, resigned.
He splashes his face with water.
He looks at the water,
and becomes entranced.
Fascinated, inspired.

DR. GIVINGS

Annie!

Annie appears.

DR. GIVINGS

Can you take this down? I have suddenly thought up a new invention.

She takes notes.

DR. GIVINGS

A vibrator made of water! The healing power of water, married to a great electrical force—could be—my goodness, revolutionary. The patient would experience a *calming* effect from the water, even as she has a release from the pressure, revitalizing the circulation. It could be used on patients who are prone to excitability—like my wife—that is to say—we will need twenty feet of copper piping right away, can you order it from the hardware store as soon as possible?

ANNIE

Yes, sir.

Annie exits.
Dr. Givings tries to work out with his
hands in the air how his invention would work.
Mrs. Givings reenters the living room with Leo.
They are laughing and their faces are flushed.

MRS. GIVINGS

How glad I am that I found you!

LEO

And I you.
You might have caught a terrible fever making snow angels without your coat—you looked like a fallen angel.

MRS. GIVINGS

Did I? Oh, I am cold, but the cold feels marvelous, I feel awake, my skin is tingling.

LEO

I must paint you like this.

MRS. GIVINGS

Leo—Mr. Irving—I must ask you—I know it is not proper—but I do not care today, I do not care at all—when you receive the treatment from my husband, where does he put it? The instrument?

LEO

I do not think your husband would like me to say, he would only speak of it in Latin or in Greek.

MRS. GIVINGS

Well, I only know English. Can you show me on my person?

LEO

Er—no. I may be an artist but I am also a gentleman.

MRS. GIVINGS

There is no such thing. Which is it, Mr. Irving? Do you dare to be an artist, or a gentleman?

She moves toward him.
He moves away.

LEO

Look at the snow, out the window. Do you not think, Mrs. Givings, that snow is always kind? Because it has to fall slowly, to meet the ground slowly, or the eyelash slowly— And things that meet each other slowly are kind.

MRS. GIVINGS

You are changing the subject.

LEO

Indeed I am.

MRS. GIVINGS

Meet me slowly, like snow.

She puts her hand on his cheek, slowly.

MRS. GIVINGS

I cannot bear it.

Dr. Givings enters the living room, yelling for Annie:

DR. GIVINGS

Wait—Annie—we'll also need ten copper valves—

He sees his wife's hand on Leo's cheek.

DR. GIVINGS

Had a good walk I trust?

Mrs. Givings takes her hand from Leo's cheek.

LEO

I discovered your wife in the snow with no coat and insisted upon
walking her home to warm her up before she caught a fever.

DR. GIVINGS

Then you did me a very great service, Mr. Irving.

LEO

Good-bye, Dr. Givings, Mrs. Givings.

DR. GIVINGS

Good-bye.

Dr. Givings turns to his wife.

DR. GIVINGS

Was your hand on his cheek?

MRS. GIVINGS

It was.

DR. GIVINGS

I see.

MRS. GIVINGS

And do you mind very much?

A pause, he considers.

DR. GIVINGS

It is odd—for some husbands such things end in a screaming match or even in death, one hand on a cheek. It has come to mean an absolute thing: the end of a book, those dreadful Mrs. Bovary books—but how can it be absolute when there are so many shades and degrees of love? Lady novelists like for it to be a tragedy— because it means that the affair mattered, mattered terribly—but it doesn't, it needn't.

MRS. GIVINGS

The writer of Madame Bovary was not a woman.

DR. GIVINGS

He was French, which is much the same thing.

MRS. GIVINGS

You dare to make a joke about the French—at this moment?
Most men would be—pale with rage!

DR. GIVINGS

Pale with rage, exactly, in a sentimental novel. My point is: this
is not the end of the book. You made a mistake, that is all. The
treatment I gave you made you excitable. It is my fault. A hand
on the cheek, these are muscles, skin, facts. It needn't mean that
one is preferred absolutely, or that one isn't loved. So why then
jealousy? My darling, I don't mind.

MRS. GIVINGS

Oh.
I had hoped that you would mind.

She storms out of the room.
Dr. Givings is left alone.

DR. GIVINGS

Catherine?

He follows after her.

MRS. GIVINGS

Don't talk to me tonight, don't talk to me tomorrow! I will take
breakfast in my own room!

A door slamming.
A song on the piano.

Second Scene

A few days later. Leo is painting Elizabeth, who is nursing Letitia.
She is dressed vaguely as the Virgin Mary, in one of Mrs. Givings's gowns.
Mrs. Givings watches Leo paint.
The painting does not face us, we do not see it.

LEO

It will be a revolution! I will call it: Nursing Madonna! How can there be so few Madonnas in which the baby Jesus actually gives suck.

MRS. GIVINGS

We are to think of Him feeding us, I suppose. Not the other way round.

Mrs. Givings gets up and paces.
She is jealous, of nursing and of being painted.
Leo goes to Elizabeth.

LEO

(To Elizabeth) Elizabeth, could you just—

He arranges the fabric so that her breast is more exposed.
Mrs. Givings examines the painting.

MRS. GIVINGS

Hmm.

LEO

Don't look at it, it's not done yet—

MRS. GIVINGS

Sorry.

LEO

Elizabeth, could you just—

He angles her head toward the baby.

LEO

There. Beautiful. There is nothing so peaceful as nursing a baby.
The baby and the mother become one being, do they not?

Mrs. Givings taps her foot.

LEO

You seem nervous, Mrs. Givings.

MRS. GIVINGS

We should stop. My husband will be home from the club shortly
and he wouldn't approve of this, not at all.

LEO

I don't see why. Your husband is a man who understands science, why then he must understand nature.

Leo resumes painting.

MRS. GIVINGS

(In low tones to Leo) I am not supposed to talk to his patients, much less arrange for them to see the bare breasts of the—help— in my living room.

LEO

Leave behind the stranglehold of convention and loosen your corset, Mrs. Givings, you will breathe much better.

ELIZABETH

She is done eating. She has fallen asleep.

He paints.
Mrs. Givings paces.

MRS. GIVINGS

I can hold the baby.

LEO

I need her there for the angle of Elizabeth's hands.

MRS. GIVINGS

Oh.
What day of the week is it, anyway?

ELIZABETH

Wednesday.

MRS. GIVINGS

That's right, Wednesday. It is always Wednesday, isn't it? Or it was Wednesday only yesterday. It is almost never Friday. It is never, ever Tuesday, but always Wednesday, I find. Smack in the middle of the week. With nothing to look forward to but the charwoman coming and cleaning out the ashes.
Are you almost done with her hands?

LEO

Hands are difficult. You would think they would be just five quick lines, but no, they have personalities as intimate as faces. Elizabeth's hands, for instance—they are fine hands, with long fingers that remind me of tapered candles. A person one has loved—the memory of their hands. Did they flutter or sit still? Dry? Moist? Cool on a hot forehead? What? That is what I wish to express in my paintings. The memory—of the movement—of very particular hands, even though they appear to be unmoving on canvas.

MRS. GIVINGS

Have you loved many women, Mr. Irving? Do you remember many—hands?

LEO

I have loved enough women to know how to paint.
If I had loved fewer, I would be an illustrator; if I had loved more, I would be a poet.

MRS. GIVINGS

Are poets required to love many women?

LEO

Oh, yes. Love animates every line.

MRS. GIVINGS

But what of the rest of us mere mortals. How many times must
we fall in love in order to live through the week.

LEO

There is also the love of God, love of country, love of children.

MRS. GIVINGS

Indeed.

LEO

I must look at her hands.

The front door opens. Leo stops painting.
Dr. Givings enters.
They startle.
Elizabeth covers her breast.
Dr. Givings is shocked at the scene in his living room.
Then he pretends he hasn't seen anything.

DR. GIVINGS

You are early for your appointment, Mr. Irving.

LEO

Yes.

DR. GIVINGS

I will wash up and see you in the operating theater.
Good afternoon, Elizabeth. *Catherine.*

He exits to the operating theater.

ELIZABETH

Oh, God.

MRS. GIVINGS

It's all right. As you see, he is a man of science. Nothing upsets or shocks him.

LEO

You talk as if that's a crime. What a capital husband you have. Completely beyond the dictates of modern society. I love your husband.

ELIZABETH

Shall I take the baby into the nuscry?

MRS. GIVINGS

Yes, that will be all, Elizabeth.
I will put the paint things away.
Go to your *appointmcnt*, Mr. Irving.

LEO

Thank you, Elizabeth. You were nothing short of divine.
Did you mind terribly being looked at? Being seen?

ELIZABETH

Who minds being seen?

LEO

Who?

ELIZABETH

Only criminals. I suppose.

LEO

Indeed.

MRS. GIVINGS

Good day, Mr. Irving.

LEO

Mrs. Givings.

Leo enters the operating theater.

DR. GIVINGS

No need to undress all the way. We can be quick about it. Just lower your trousers.

Meanwhile, Mrs. Givings tries to hide the painting in the living room.

DR. GIVINGS

It seems that you and my wife are becoming acquinated.

LEO

A bit.

DR. GIVINGS

I see. She's a wonderful woman, is she not?

LEO

Yes.

DR. GIVINGS

I'm a lucky man.

Dr. Givings inserts the Chattanooga vibrator, a little more firmly than usual.

DR. GIVINGS

And your health, it seems to be much improved?

LEO

Yes, I am painting again. In fact, I cannot stop painting.

DR. GIVINGS

How wonderful. I am so glad for you.

Leo has an anal paroxysm.

LEO

Oh.

DR. GIVINGS

I do think you're cured now.
We can stop the treatments.

LEO

Thank you, Doctor.
I believe you've saved my life.

Dr. Givings puts away the vibrator.

LEO

I am suddenly drowsy.

DR. GIVINGS

Take a nap.
Good day.

Dr. Givings exits to his private study.
Leo drowses.

In the living room:

The doorbell rings.
Mrs. Givings answers the door.
Mr. and Mrs. Daldry enter.

MRS. GIVINGS

Ah, Mr. and Mrs. Daldry!

MR. AND MRS. DALDRY

Hello.

MRS. GIVINGS

I have not visited with you since it was raining, Mr. Daldry.

MR. DALDRY

And I have not seen you since you were wet.
Have you been well?
You look well.
Very well.

MRS. GIVINGS

Thank you.

MR. DALDRY

It's good you're done with that odious nursing business. A woman
like you should be—enjoying yourself—not shut up in a nursery
all day.

MRS. DALDRY

(To Mr. Daldry) Will you do me a favor, my dear, and take a walk
around the grounds before my appointment?
I wish to speak to Mrs. Givings about my needlework before Dr.
Givings arrives and I fear we'll bore you.

MR. DALDRY

I don't have much to say on the subject of needlepoint. I'll see you
shortly. Darling. Mrs. Givings.

MRS. GIVINGS

(As he moves to the door) Take a left turn by the fountain—there is
a winter garden—I planted it myself—

MR. DALDRY

I didn't know anything grew in winter—

MRS. GIVINGS

Oh, yes—juniper and periwinkle and—

MR. DALDRY

It's all the same to me. But if you planted it, Mrs. Givings, I'm
sure it's lovely.

He exits.

MRS. DALDRY

I wanted to speak with you.

MRS. GIVINGS

Come and sit. You have taken up needlework?

MRS. DALDRY

No. I hate needlework. I have been thinking about what you said—
about having two experiences of the same event.
I want very much to—I do not know how to—
but I was thinking—if we go into the operating
theater again, and if we place the instrument just so—
and if you held it, and then I held it—but we did a kind of—

Mrs. Daldry gestures, oddly.
Elizabeth enters.

ELIZABETH

I laid her down to sleep in her pram. I am sorry about the—

MRS. GIVINGS

Never mind, Elizabeth.
You may go now.
Wait, Elizabeth, before you leave—
perhaps you can settle a question.
Mrs. Daldry and I have had two experiences of the very same event.
Have you ever had this sensation?
Either: you have shivers all over your body, and you feel like
running, and your feet get very hot, as though you are dancing
on devil's coals—

MRS. DALDRY

Or you see unaccountable patterns of light, of electricity, under
your eyelids—and your heart races—and your legs feel very weak,
as though you cannot walk—

MRS. GIVINGS

Or your face gets suddenly hot, like a strange sudden sunburn—

MRS. DALDRY

Or there are red splotches up one side of your entire body—a
strange rash—here—

She points to her chest.

MRS. GIVINGS

And the feeling of burning, as though you'll get no relief—and
your mouth is dry and you have to lick your lips—and you find
your face making a very ugly expression, so you cover your face
with your hands—

MRS. DALDRY

And sometimes a great outpouring of liquid, and the sheets are wet, but it is not an unpleasant sensation, only a little frightening?

ELIZABETH

Is that a riddle?

MRS. GIVINGS

Has that ever happened to you?

ELIZABETH

I do not know—the sensations are so contradictory. Does anything unite them?

MRS. GIVINGS

Many of them are—down below.

ELIZABETH

Oh—I see.
Well, the things you describe, some of them seem to be sensations that an invalid would have, or someone with a horrible fever—but others—sound like sensations that women might have when they are having relations with their husbands.

A pause.

ELIZABETH

I'm sorry. Perhaps you were joking. Perhaps—I shouldn't have said—

MRS. GIVINGS

With their husbands?

MRS. DALDRY

How interesting.

ELIZABETH

Those sensations you are describing—they are not from having relations with your husbands?

MRS. DALDRY

Good heavens, no!

MRS. GIVINGS

No! Good God.

They laugh.

MRS. DALDRY

I don't know what I should do if I felt those things in the presence of my husband—I'd be so embarrassed I would leave the room immediately. As it is—my husband is very considerate—when he comes to my room at night, I am asleep—he tells me to keep my eyes shut, and I do—so I feel only the darkness—and then the pain—I lie very still—I do not see his face—my husband is—has always been—very considerate.

MRS. GIVINGS

Of course.

MRS. DALDRY

But the instrument produces a very different kind of pain, does it not? Very different from the other kind of pain? With my husband—

Leo enters the room, a bit dazed.

LEO

Ladies.

They nod to him.
Elizabeth is embarrassed to see him.

ELIZABETH

Good-bye then.

LEO

(To Elizabeth) I will see you home.
I have a good enough likeness, I can finish the painting at my studio.

ELIZABETH

I can walk home myself.

LEO

No, I wouldn't hear of it, I will walk you home.

ELIZABETH

No thank you, Mr. Irving.

LEO

Please. You did me a great service today, I can at least see that you
get home.

MRS. GIVINGS

(To Leo) Oh, don't go just yet!

LEO

I'll just see Elizabeth home. Oh, the painting!

MRS. GIVINGS

I'll get it.

She hands him the painting.
Elizabeth exits.

MRS. GIVINGS

I will see you soon?

LEO

I'm afraid my treatments are at an end. I'm cured.

MRS. GIVINGS

But that's impossible!

*Dr. Givings enters from the operating theater
and sees the good-bye between Leo and Catherine.*

LEO

I will see you again. Never fear. Good-bye, Catherine. *(He takes
her hand, then sees Dr. Givings, and drops it)* Dr. Givings. Farewell.

Leo runs out the door.

DR. GIVINGS

Mrs. Daldry. I did not hear you arrive. I'll just let you get ready.

*Mrs. Daldry moves to the operating theater
and undresses with the help of Annie.*

In the living room:

DR. GIVINGS

What can you be thinking of? Do you mean to embarrass me?

MRS. GIVINGS

I thought it was only a scene in a book to you. Or a fact.

DR. GIVINGS

Do you think it's escaped my notice that you haven't breakfasted
with me for five days running?

MRS. GIVINGS

Breakfast is not a very romantic meal. I decided to skip it.

DR. GIVINGS

Is every meal supposed to be romantic?

MRS. GIVINGS

I do not enjoy you silently reading your scientific journals while
I eat my toast.

DR. GIVINGS

You prefer grand passions over toast? My God, woman, we are
married, a man needs to be quiet at least once a day.

MRS. GIVINGS

So I'll be quiet then! HERE I AM! QUIET! QUIET AS A
MOUSE!

Mr. Daldry enters the living room.

MR. DALDRY

What a beautiful winter garden—sorry, am I interrupting?

MRS. GIVINGS

No. We were just discussing breakfast. You know, in Italy they
hardly eat breakfast. Just a little bit of sweet cracker to dip in very
strong coffee. They eat something light to recover from the great
passions they spent during the night. Better to skip breakfast and
move on to lunch, a great big lunch, when the silence isn't quite so
loud, no the silence is not quite so deafening at lunch.

DR. GIVINGS

How do you know about biscotti?

MRS. GIVINGS

Mr. Irving told me.

DR. GIVINGS

I see.

MR. DALDRY

I know nothing about biscotti. I like ham and eggs for breakfast, sausage too. A big breakfast is important for one's energy, Mrs. Givings. I have once heard it said that small women should eat large animals. You ought to eat a bit of meat for breakfast, some bacon, or some sausage.

MRS. GIVINGS

Oh, I have plenty of energy, Mr. Daldry. I don't need to borrow energy from a cow. I have so much energy I do not know what to do with it, you see.

MR. DALDRY

Mmmm.

Annie sticks her head in the living room:

ANNIE

We're ready for you, Doctor.

DR. GIVINGS

Will you excuse me.

MRS. GIVINGS AND MR. DALDRY

(An approximation of) Oh, yes, certainly.

Dr. Givings enters the operating theater.
He is distracted.
He puts the vibrator on Mrs. Daldry's torso.

MRS. DALDRY

Dr. Givings?

DR. GIVINGS

Yes?

MRS. DALDRY

Is something wrong?

DR. GIVINGS

Oh—terribly sorry. I am distracted.

He moves the vibrator.
In the living room, Mr. Daldry and Mrs. Givings sit on the couch.
He moves toward her.

MR. DALDRY

Mrs. Givings. I—don't always know how to converse—in a drawing room. I—

He tries to kiss her.
She slaps him.

MRS. GIVINGS

Mr. Daldry!
What can you be thinking of?

MR. DALDRY

You said about your energies. I thought—

MRS. GIVINGS

You insult me.

MR. DALDRY

You have no idea how I long for a woman of energy. My wife is so tired, she is so tired, all the time.

MRS. GIVINGS

How dare you speak ill of your wife in my presence. Go. Please.

MR. DALDRY

Will you have the goodness to tell Mrs. Daldry to meet me at home, I will send a carriage for her.

Mrs. Givings nods.
Mr. Daldry leaves.
She goes to the door of the operating theater and hesitates there, sinking down, upset.

DR. GIVINGS

It has been taking longer with you of late. Perhaps I need to build a new instrument with a few more beats per minute—perhaps the body gets accustomed to so many beats per minute and then requires more—

He adjusts the vibrator.

DR. GIVINGS

Hmm. Nothing. Is it past three minutes?

He looks at his pocket watch.

MRS. DALDRY

Perhaps if Annie tries.

DR. GIVINGS

Yes, of course, Annie why don't you have a go. I will attend to some business.

Annie takes the vibrator and tries.
Dr. Givings leaves the room.
He almost trips on his wife at the door.

DR. GIVINGS

My God. You are acting the part of a madwoman in a play!
Listening at doors?

MRS. GIVINGS

You will offer to her what you deny to me!

DR. GIVINGS

It is *medicine*, my love!

MRS. GIVINGS

And I say it isn't!

DR. GIVINGS

I thought I heard a slap!

MRS. GIVINGS

It was nothing, nothing at all.

Mrs. Daldry has a louder than usual paroxysm.
They both hear it.

MRS. GIVINGS

Well, your work is done now.
You can go to the club.
And argue about the benefits of the alternating current over and
above the direct current.

DR. GIVINGS

And you?
Do you favor the alternating or direct?

MRS. GIVINGS

Direct. From here to here.

She gestures from his heart to her heart.

DR. GIVINGS

Interesting. I would have guessed alternating. More complicated, changing direction dozens of times per second. Faces slapped by nobody. Italian breakfasts. Etcetera. I'll be at the club.

He exits.
Mrs. Givings moves toward the operating theater.
Annie and Mrs. Daldry are sitting in a weirdly compromised postcoital state of reflection.

MRS. DALDRY

Annie, have you ever used the instrument upon yourself?

ANNIE

Oh, no. For I've never been ill. I've scarcely had a day's illness in my life. Maybe a bit of a stomach bug, but nothing mental. I'm sound as a horse, I was raised on a farm.

MRS. DALDRY

I could hold the instrument on you, if you would like, it is not unpleasant, and perhaps it would be interesting for you to experience it.

ANNIE

I do not think the doctor would like it.

Mrs. Givings enters the operating theater.

MRS. GIVINGS

My husband . . . has gone to the club. And Mr. Daldry has also left.
He sent a carriage for you. They both said their farewells.

MRS. DALDRY

Thank you, Mrs. Givings.

MRS. GIVINGS

Shall I leave you?
I could—

A suspended moment in which
we are not sure if we might witness
three women playing with the vibrator together.
All of them think about it.
They all look at one another, and then at the instrument.

MRS. DALDRY

I—

ANNIE

I—

MRS. DALDRY

I must get dressed.

MRS. GIVINGS

Of course. Annie, do you need any assistance cleaning up?

ANNIE

No, thank you, Mrs. Givings. It's very easy to clean up.

MRS. GIVINGS

All right then.
I will leave you.

Mrs. Givings exits.
Annie helps Mrs. Daldry get dressed.

MRS. DALDRY

Well.

ANNIE

Well, then.

MRS. DALDRY

I suppose we could—continue with my Greek lesson.

ANNIE

Oh, yes. I believe we left off with the early Greek philosophers. Thales thought the earth was suspended on water, floated there, and he thought that all magnets had souls because they moved towards one another.

MRS. DALDRY

I can well believe that magnets have souls. When I look into dark eyes, like magnets, I am moved, unaccountably. You have very dark eyes, like magnets—has any man ever told you so?

ANNIE

No man has told me much aside from: pass the clamp.

MRS. DALDRY

They should Annie, they really should. Whatever happened to Thales?

ANNIE

He never married. His mother told him he should marry and he said: it's too early. And when she pressed him again, ten years later, he said: it's too late.

MRS. DALDRY

And you? Why have you never married?

ANNIE

One day, I woke up, and it was too late.

MRS. DALDRY

I see.

Annie, I have been thinking. I wonder whether I could purchase one of these instruments for home use. The doctor is so busy, and I really feel I'm almost better. My color has returned, and I wake up in the morning and feel hopeful. I could use it only as required, when, for example, I have trouble sleeping, as I often do, and I can't very well call on the doctor past midnight.

ANNIE

Well—it might be dangerous for home use, because of the potential for electrocution, but I will ask the doctor. You know he is very open to inventions.

MRS. DALDRY

I would be too embarrassed to ask.

ANNIE

I will ask for you.

MRS. DALDRY

Good-bye then, Annie

ANNIE

Good-bye.

MRS. DALDRY

Thank you, Annie.

ANNIE

For what?

MRS. DALDRY

For the Greek lesson.

Mrs. Daldry exits.
Annie washes her hands.
She looks at the vibrator, thinks of using it on herself,
thinks better of it, puts it away.

Meanwhile, Mrs. Givings is lying on the sofa in the living room.

MRS. DALDRY

Are you quite all right, Mrs. Givings? Your color looks off.

MRS. GIVINGS

I am not myself.

MRS. DALDRY

Is there anything I can do?

MRS. GIVINGS

No, thank you.
Mrs. Daldry, did you dream of love from a young age?

MRS. DALDRY

Yes.

MRS. GIVINGS

And what did you think it would be like?

MRS. DALDRY

I thought it would be—never wanting for anything. Being surrounded and lifted up. Like resting on water, for eternity.

MRS. GIVINGS

And is that what you have found in marriage?

MRS. DALDRY

There have been moments of rest. But as it turns out, the earth rests on air, not on water, and the air can feel very—insubstantial—at times. Even though it is holding you up, invisibly.

MRS. GIVINGS

Yes.

MRS. DALDRY

Do you mind if I play your piano?

MRS. GIVINGS

Oh, please do.

Mrs. Daldry plays the piano, full of longing.
From offstage, the baby cries.

MRS. GIVINGS

Excuse me.

Mrs. Givings exits to attend to the baby.
Annie enters and listens to Mrs Daldry play.
Annie goes to sit beside Mrs. Daldry on the piano bench.
Mrs. Daldry finishes the song.
Annie claps.
They kiss.

MRS. DALDRY

What?

ANNIE

Oh.

MRS. DALDRY

How strange.

ANNIE

Oh dear.

MRS. DALDRY

I had better not see you ever again.

ANNIE

I suppose not.

MRS. DALDRY

Good-bye then Annie.

ANNIE

Good-bye.

Mrs. Daldry exits.
Mrs. Givings enters.

MRS. GIVINGS

Annie?

ANNIE

What a sad song she played. I believe it made me tear up a little.
Good-bye Mrs. Givings.

MRS. GIVINGS

Oh, don't leave, Annie—Dr. Givings is at the club and I have very
little company.

ANNIE

I'm afraid I must go.

MRS. GIVINGS

What is the matter?

ANNIE

That song made me sad. Good-bye.

Mrs. Givings, alone.
The doorbell rings.
Elizabeth enters, not entirely herself.

MRS. GIVINGS

Elizabeth. I did not expect you. What is it?

ELIZABETH

Mrs. Givings, I came to tell you that today was my last day working for you. My husband doesn't like me gone so much. He wants me home with my own children.

MRS. GIVINGS

But you can't leave us, Elizabeth! What on earth will we do without you?

ELIZABETH

She is almost ready to have cow's milk. Or a little bit of rice porridge.

MRS. GIVINGS

I suppose. I was not thinking only of the food.

Elizabeth nods slowly.

MRS. GIVINGS

But why today? I don't understand.

ELIZABETH

Mr. Irving insisted on walking me home. He was not—inappropriate—but he kept hold of my arm. He paid me a large sum of money—for the sitting. And he walked me up to my front door.

MRS. GIVINGS

Oh, dear.

ELIZABETH

My husband was home. My husband saw him. And me. And the painting.

MRS. GIVINGS

Oh! Was your husband very angry? About the painting?

ELIZABETH

The painting? No. He cried when he saw the painting. It's your hands, he said. Mr. Irving must be a good painter, it's hard to paint hands.
But he doesn't want me working here, not anymore.

MRS. GIVINGS

Of course. Yes—I understand.

ELIZABETH

No—you don't.

A pause.

ELIZABETH

I'll just say good-bye to Lotty. I have grown fond of her.

MRS. GIVINGS

Yes. Well.

She is in the nursery. She is fat and happy, all thanks to you.

Elizabeth—how old was your Henry Douglas when he died?

ELIZABETH

Twelve weeks.

MRS. GIVINGS

What did he die of?

ELIZABETH

Cholera.

MRS. GIVINGS

I am sorry.

ELIZABETH

Thank you.

MRS. GIVINGS

I think I should die of sorrow, in your place.

ELIZABETH

Die of sorrow? A mother of two cannot die of sorrow.

MRS. GIVINGS

But how do you go on, after?

ELIZABETH

My mother told me to pray each day since I was a little girl, to pray
that you borrow everything, everyone you love, from God. That
way your heart doesn't break when you have to give your son, or
your mother, or your husband, back to God. I prayed, Jesus, let

me be humble. I borrowed my child, I borrowed my husband, I borrowed my own life from you, God. But he felt like *mine* not like God's he felt like *mine* more mine than anything.

God must have this huge horrible cabinet—all the babies who get returned—and all those babies inside, they're all crying even with God Himself to rock them to sleep, still they want their mothers. So when I started to feel something for this baby, for your baby, I thought no, take her back God.

When I first met her all I could think was: she is alive and Henry is not. I had all this milk—I wished it would dry up. Just get through the year, I thought. Your milk will dry up and you will forget. The more healthy your baby got, the more dead my baby became. I thought of her like a tick. I thought—fill her up and then pop! You will see the blood of my Henry underneath. But she seemed so grateful for the milk. Sometimes I hated her for it. But she would look at me, she would give me this look—I do not know what to call it if it is not called love. I hope every day you keep her—you keep her close to you—and you remember the blood that her milk was made from. The blood of my son, my Henry. Good-bye, Mrs. Givings.

MRS. GIVINGS

Good-bye, Elizabeth.

Mrs. Givings touches Elizabeth's elbow.
Elizabeth nods.
Elizabeth pulls away and exits, to the nursery.

MRS. GIVINGS

Thank you.

But Elizabeth is out the door.
Mrs. Givings, alone.

She moves toward the operating theater.
The doorbell rings.
It is Leo.

MRS. GIVINGS

You have made quite a mess of things for Elizabeth.

LEO

I know. I'm sorry. I've come to say good-bye.
I'm moving to Paris.

MRS. GIVINGS

When?

LEO

Tomorrow.

MRS. GIVINGS

Take me with you.

LEO

Are you out of your mind?

MRS. GIVINGS

You are surprised? It was you who seduced me!

LEO

What?

MRS. GIVINGS

All that talk of women, two-thirds done, that was me, you were
talking of me, were you not?

LEO

I was talking of paintings. I—

MRS. GIVINGS

No one has ever spoken to me of those things before. Of beauty—of prostitutes, of—my God, of *Italy*. How could I have misunderstood your intentions? I'm in love with you.

LEO

Oh, dear Catherine I am afraid I cannot love you. If there is any type to whom I am attracted—it veers toward women with doe eyes. And your eyes are more—they are more—thin—the light bounces off of them rather than into them. And I cannot see your soul hovering here, where I would like to. Your soul is locked somewhere inside your body, so I cannot see it. Another man could perhaps bring your soul outside your eyes but it's not me, I'm afraid. I do care for you though.

MRS. GIVINGS

Try. Try to bring my soul out—to here. If you look into my eyes—see—I will try.
Are you bringing another woman with you?

LEO

No—I am going alone.
Don't you see? It is Elizabeth who I love.

MRS. GIVINGS

Elizabeth?

LEO

Yes.

MRS. GIVINGS

Oh—I see nothing, I understand nothing—my God, Elizabeth.

LEO

Yes. And she doesn't care for me, not at all. I told her of my
affections on our walk and she slapped me. No—I will go to Paris
alone. I am married to my solitude.

MRS. GIVINGS

I can be your solitude. I will be quiet as a mouse. I understand
solitude, I am very lonely.

LEO

I do not understand your loneliness, Mrs. Givings. You have a
child, a husband—a *home*!

MRS. GIVINGS

Yes. I am very ungrateful. I am sure that God will punish me.

She tries to embrace him.

LEO

No. You do not love me. You only think you do. You love your
husband. He is a good man. Good-bye, now.

He kisses her hands.

MRS. GIVINGS

Elizabeth is in the nursery. If you wish to say good-bye to her.

LEO

I can't bear to see her. Just give her this, won't you?

Leo kisses Mrs. Givings on the cheek.

LEO

Come visit me in France. I promise you—you'll love the paintings.

He leaves.
She goes into the operating theater.
She plugs in the vibrator.
She puts it to her private parts but
she is too sad for it to work.
She cries as it hums along.
Dr. Givings enters.

DR. GIVINGS

My dear, what on earth are you doing?

MRS. GIVINGS

(Bawling) I am alone.

DR. GIVINGS

You are not alone, I am here. Have you been using this instrument on yourself?

Dr. Givings shuts off the vibrator.

MRS. GIVINGS

I am so lonely—Elizabeth is leaving us—Leo is leaving us— everyone is leaving—you are gone—you are at the club, or in the next room, always in the next room, with the door locked. You see that women are capable of pressing a button themselves.

DR. GIVINGS

Darling—

MRS. GIVINGS

When you touched them, the other women, and Leo, with the machine, did you feel love for them, when you touched them there, was it like love?

DR. GIVINGS

No. I only wanted them to feel better.

MRS. GIVINGS

And when you married me, did you want to love me, or did you
want to make me feel better?

DR. GIVINGS

A doctor wants to make everyone feel better.

MRS. GIVINGS

But did you want to love me?

DR. GIVINGS

Yes! And you—with your hands on other men's faces—do you
love them? Do you love Mr. Irving?

MRS. GIVINGS

A little.

DR. GIVINGS

I have a strange feeling in my stomach.

MRS. GIVINGS

What is it?

DR. GIVINGS

My eyes feel funny and my stomach feels jumpy. I believe I'm
jealous.

MRS. GIVINGS

Give up your operating theater, darling.

DR. GIVINGS

And do what instead?

MRS. GIVINGS

Love me. Love me for your job.

DR. GIVINGS

All day long?

MRS. GIVINGS

All day long. I have heard that some women do not need the vibrating instrument to give them paroxysms, that relations with their husbands have much the same effect. Love me for your job.

DR. GIVINGS

I would like to love you.

MRS. GIVINGS

Would you?

DR. GIVINGS

Yes. I have not known how.

MRS. GIVINGS

You said to me when my hand was on another man's cheek that there were all types and shades of love—But what is it then, this very particular way in which you love me? What color? What temperature? And please do not say: you are my wife, I am your husband.

DR. GIVINGS

I do not have the words.

MRS. GIVINGS

Please try.

DR. GIVINGS

That is why they have poets—to classify all the degrees of love. It is for scientists to classify the maladies arising from the want of it.

MRS. GIVINGS

Try.

DR. GIVINGS

Do not make fun of me. Do you promise?

MRS. GIVINGS

I promise.

DR. GIVINGS

(Kissing tenderly each place as he names it—all on the face)
I bless thee: temporomandibular joint
I bless thee: buccal artery and nerve
I bless thee: depressor anguli oris
I bless thee: zygomatic arch
I bless thee: temporalis fascia.

I bless thee, Catherine.

Mrs. Givings cries, it is so intimate.

MRS. GIVINGS

Open me.

DR. GIVINGS

Here?

MRS. GIVINGS

Away from the machine.
In the garden.
Undress me there.

DR. GIVINGS

You wish to undress in the garden in December?

MRS. GIVINGS

Yes, and please,
do not call me impractical. Our whole
future happiness depends upon it.

Dr. and Mrs. Givings kiss.
Although the domestic space seemed terribly permanent—a settee, a
statuette—suddenly it disappears and we are in a sweet small winter
garden. Snow covers trees that in the spring flower with pink flowers.

MRS. GIVINGS

Undress me.
Do not close your eyes, look at me . . .

He undresses her, partially.

DR. GIVINGS

The street lamps are coming on. Someone will see us.

MRS. GIVINGS

No one will see. They are not electric yet.
Thank God something still flickers.

She undresses him.

MRS. GIVINGS

Are you cold?

DR. GIVINGS

No. Are you cold?

MRS. GIVINGS

No.

We don't need to see all of his body,
it is dark out—
but we do see the moon glowing off his skin,
off his back and shoulders.
He need not face us.
She has never seen him naked before—
she has only seen him under the covers.

MRS. GIVINGS

How beautiful you are! Your body!
I have never before seen that little bit there, under the covers—
or that bit there, or this beautiful line here—
I have felt this shadow there but I have never seen it—
how it curves—

Pointing to different lines on his body.

DR. GIVINGS

I am embarrassed.

MRS. GIVINGS

Don't be.
Lie down and make a snow angel.

He lies on his back and makes an angel in the snow.
She lies on top of him.
They make an angel.
They make their wings go back and forth.
It snows on them.

Outside, on the street corners, the gas lamps go on, one by one,
flickering, insubstantial.

DR. GIVINGS

Catherine.

MRS. GIVINGS

Oh, God. Oh, God, Oh, God.

And the rest of the lights go out.
The end.

Music

I am happy to include Jonathan Bell's beautiful music from the Lincoln Center production. Of course future productions are welcome to compose their own music, but I thought this would be helpful for readers and listeners who want to imagine the musical tone of the piece. If you wish to use Jonathan's music for a production, please contact him at jblingaling@gmail.com.

In The Next Room- "Bird House" Song (Act 1, Sc. 2)

Jonathan Bell

In The Next Room- "Sad" Piece (Act 1, Sc. 2)

Jonathan Bell

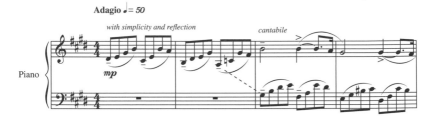

In The Next Room- "Kiss" Piece (Act 2, Sc. 2)

Jonathan Bell

Lento con Moto ♩= *80*

Acknowledgments

I would like to thank New Dramatists and some wonderful actors who helped me in the workshop phase of this play: Eisa Davis, Carla Harting, Reed Birney, Mary Catherine Garrison, Michael Esper, Amy Warren, Marin Ireland, and the whole cast of *Eurydice*. Thanks to Kathleen Chalfant for loaning us her living room when we read the very first draft of this play. Thank you to André Bishop and Bernie Gersten for believing the play could survive on Broadway. Thanks to all the designers: Annie, David, Russell, Bray and Jonanthan for being genius collaborators. Thank you to Paula Vogel, Anne Cattaneo, Madeleine Oldham and Denise Bilbao for reading early drafts; and to Tina Howe, Kathleen Tolan, Andy Bragen, Crystal Finn, Kate Pines, Sarah Rasmussen, Roy Harris, Denise Yaney, Vanessa Poggioli and David Adjmi for helping me get through previews. And many many thanks to Les Waters, without whom this play would never have been written, and to the original cast in Berkeley—Paul (also for your generosity revisiting the play), Hannah, Joaquín, Maria, Stacy, John and Melle—for so bravely finding the play's voice. And to the cast at the Lyceum—Laura, Michael, Maria, Chandler, Tom, Quincy, Wendy—some of my favorite moments of theater were simply watching you all rehearse.

SARAH RUHL's plays include *In the Next Room or the vibrator play* (Glickman Prize, finalist for the 2010 Pulitzer Prize, nominee for the Tony Award for Best Play), *The Clean House* (The Susan Smith Blackburn Award, 2004; finalist for the Pulitzer Prize, 2005), *Dead Man's Cell Phone* (Helen Hayes Award for Best New Play), *Demeter in the City* (nominated for nine NAACP awards), *Eurydice*, *Melancholy Play*, *Orlando*, *Late: a cowboy song* and *Passion Play* (Kennedy Center's The Fourth Freedom Forum Playwriting Award). Her plays have premiered on Broadway at the Lyceum Theater (produced by Lincoln Center Theater); Off-Broadway at Lincoln Center Theater, Playwrights Horizons, Second Stage Theatre; and regionally at Berkeley Repertory Theatre, Yale Repertory Theatre, the Goodman Theatre, Cornerstone Theater Company, Arena Stage, Woolly Mammoth Theatre, the Piven Theatre; as well as being produced at many other theaters across the country. Her plays have also been performed in England, Poland, Germany, Israel, New Zealand and Australia, and have been translated into Spanish, Polish, Russian, Korean and Arabic. Sarah received her MFA from Brown University, where she studied with Paula Vogel, and is originally from Chicago. In 2003, she was the recipient of a Helen Merrill Emerging Playwrights Award, a Whiting Writers' Award, and a PEN/Laura Pels Award; in 2006 she was the recipient of a MacArthur Fellowship. Her work is published by TCG and Samuel French, and she is a member of New Dramatists and 13P. She lives in New York City with her family.